Building
with
Water

Dedicated to Brenda, Max and Amy Ryan

Zoë Ryan

Building with Water

CONCEPTS | TYPOLOGY | DESIGN

Birkhäuser
Basel

Graphic design: Oliver Kleinschmidt, Berlin

Editor: Ria Stein, Berlin

Cover: Casa en la Barranca, Architect Rafael Iglesia, Santa Fe, Argentina

Photographer: Gustavo Frittegotto, Rosario, Argentina

Lithography: Licht + Tiefe, Berlin

Printing: Medialis, Berlin

Library of Congress Control Number: 2010923932

Bibliographic information published by the German National Library: The German National
Library lists this publication in the Deutsche Nationalbibliografie; detailed bibliographic data
is available on the Internet at http://dnb.d-nb.de.

© 2010 Birkhäuser GmbH
Basel
P.O.Box 133, CH-4010 Basel, Switzerland
Printed on acid-free paper produced from chlorine-free pulp. TCF ∞
Printed in Germany

ISBN 978-3-0346-0156-6

www.birkhauser-architecture.com

9 8 7 6 5 4 3 2 1

Content

Introduction
Fluid Dynamics: Building on Water

Sandro Botticelli, "The Birth of Venus", 1485.

Caspar David Friedrich, "Wanderer above the Sea of Fog", 1818.

J. M. W. Turner, "The Slave Ship", 1840.

Water is essential to life in every form. One of the world's most valuable resources, it has been referred to as "blue oil".[1] A material that we are forever trying to preserve, conserve, clean and re-use, water is also an element we continue to fight against, barricading ourselves, for example, against rising sea levels and the threat of flood. Given the increasing emphasis on environmental approaches to living, working and playing, water has become central to discussions about new architecture and urban planning. It is, therefore, a particularly pertinent time to be discussing building on water and the many thought-provoking and experimental projects that architects, designers and engineers are initiating that aim to address these important issues in an effort to introduce new modes of thinking and practices that will radically change our relationship with this natural resource.

Water as a Symbol

The importance of water as a source and symbol of life goes without saying. Drawn to it for its life-supporting, playful and therapeutic qualities, we cannot exist without it. Although water covers about two-thirds of the earth's surface, only 3 percent of this amount is freshwater and about two-thirds of that is ice. Much of the remainder is locked underground. Therefore, a mere fraction of 1 percent of earth's water supports all life on land. It is this essential ratio of water that provides sustenance to all forms of life and is fundamental to social development. As Flemish chemist, physiologist and physician J. Baptist van Helmont wrote in his volume *Oriatrike or Physick Refined*, published posthumously in 1662, "All earth, clay, and every body that may be touched, is truly and materially the offspring of water only, and is reduced again into water, by nature and art ..."[2]

Water appears throughout religion, literature and art of every culture. In the religious world, water is sacrosanct – from baptisms in the river Jordan to the ritual immersion in the Ganges during religious festivals in India. Spring water is also venerated. From ancient Bath in England to the modern Floridian hot springs, this natural water source is considered beneficial to physical purification and spiritual rejuvenation. As attested by Sandro Botticelli's 1485 painting "The Birth of Venus", in which Venus rises out of the sea in a scallop-shaped shell, appearing to derive her seductive power from the water, fresh and clear water is equated with health and beauty.

Counter to the life-supporting properties of this elemental material, water can also threaten and even take life. The German Romantic painter Caspar David Friedrich (1744 – 1840) illustrated man's powerlessness in the face of nature in "Wanderer above the Sea of Fog" of 1818 in which a solitary man looks out over a vast rough sea. Two decades later, J. M. W. Turner portrayed the dangers of the sea in "The Slave Ship", painted in 1840, in addition to making a marked political commentary on the practice of slavery. More recently installation artists such as Olafur Eliasson have turned to urban waterways as a source of inspiration and discovery in an effort to further awareness of the inherent relationship between water and the built environment. In 2008 he created "The New York City Waterfalls". Three falls consisting of approximately 27 to 36 metre-high scaffolding poles were installed in sites along the East River, viewable from Lower Manhattan. Torrents of water pumped up from the East River cascaded down the structures to thunderous effect. Like many of Eliasson's projects, the falls encouraged exploration of the water's edge and illustrated the power of this natural waterway, its constantly changing state and its presence in the city.

Trevi Fountain, Rome, Italy, 1762.

Water in Public Spaces

The consideration of some historical examples of interactions with this natural resource help us to fully understand our relationship with water. Charles Moore credits the city of Rome as the first to fully explore the potential for new relationships between the built environment and water with projects such as the Trevi Fountain in Rome, completed in 1762 and designed by architect Nicola Salvi. The Greek God Oceanus stands strong at the centre of a triumphal arch guarding the well, as the mythic protector of the sea and a godfather to the Greek pantheon. The circulation of the water cascading from above, collecting in the basin below and then shooting back up stands as a powerful metaphor of the natural cycle of life. As Moore notes, "All around, water splashes, foams, churns, spits, caresses stone reefs, and, at night, its luminous sparkles dance on the façades of neighbouring stone walls, windows and medieval arcades. The Trevi is the ultimate joining of water and architecture."[3] Fountains have since come to characterize many of the most famous gathering spaces from the Champs Élysées (1724) in Paris and London's Trafalgar Square (1845), to Chicago's Grant Park (1901).

Fountains continue to revitalize public spaces. In France, the Floodable Square in Bordeaux, situated on the Quai de la Douane has been surprising unsuspecting passers-by since its completion in 2006. Designed by landscape architects Atelier R and water feature designers JML, a shallow pool of water periodically floods the plaza and then recedes, disappearing within minutes, without a trace. Known for the Buckingham Fountain (1927), one of the largest in the world, Chicago's Grant Park is now also home to the Crown Fountain. An altogether different experience, this fountain, designed by Spanish artist Jaume Plensa and installed in 2004, is one of the most popular outdoor attractions in the city's downtown area. Located in Millennium Park, adjacent to the Chicago Art Institute, the water feature attracts scores of adults and children. Water cascades down the media walls that flank either side of the plaza, creating a shallow pool suitable for paddling. The faces of 2,000 Chicago residents animate the media walls. At sporadic intervals, water shoots out of the mouths of the faces to the delight, and at times dismay, of unaware pedestrians.

Revitalizing the Waterfront

Urban waterfronts have become fertile areas for urban planning and redevelopment as a key part of rebuilding healthy cities. Throughout history, canals, rivers, lakes, seas and oceans forming an edge to or bisecting urban metropolises have determined the topographical character of urban areas. Used for defense, trade, transportation, industry and recreation, these bodies of water often provided a reason for founding a city in the first place and have come to define these cities and play a major role in their lively and unique characters.

The most significant event to affect cities was the development of mercantile cities such as New York, London, Rotterdam, Chicago, Lisbon, Rio de Janeiro and Cape Town into industrial ports in the 19th century. As steam-powered boats transported goods faster and in larger quantities to ports globally, many of the world's urban waterfronts took on an industrial character with warehouses, docks and wooden piers. In addition to the potential hazards of machinery from heavy industry, these areas of intense activity suffered from high levels of pollution, making them uninhabitable as well as unsuitable for recreational activities. A disconnect grew between the waterfront and the social, cultural and environmental life of the city.

Olafur Eliasson, "The New York City Waterfalls"
(artist rendering), an installation of four man-made
waterfalls in New York, USA, 2008.

Floodable Square, Bordeaux, France,
Atelier R and JML, 2006.

Crown Fountain, Chicago, Illinois, USA,
Jaume Plensa, 2004.

Georges Seurat, "A Sunday on La Grande Jatte", 1884–1886.

Brighton Pier in Brighton, Sussex, England, opened in 1899. The pier continues to be one of the city's most popular tourist attractions.

As a contrast to these conditions, retreats on the waterfront located within easy reach of the city became fashionable as weekend destinations for city dwellers. In Georges Seurat's now well-known painting from 1884–1886, "A Sunday on La Grande Jatte", he depicts the popularity of an island in the river Seine on the outskirts of Paris for fishing, boating, picnicking and promenading. Across Northern Europe seaside resorts developed in response to changing lifestyles and increased leisure time for working families. Brighton on the southern coast of England, built under Royal supervision, introduced an architectural language that was to be replicated across Europe as a model for future resorts. With majestic architecture, boulevards and seaside promenades, the city also became famed for its 525-metre-long pier, opened in 1823, which continues to offer attractions such as a Ferris wheel. In 1841 the first railway line to Brighton extended the town's reach of influence beyond the local area. Working class families from cities such as London could now make the day trip. In the second half of the 19th century, other cities followed suit including Coney Island near New York and Atlantic City, New Jersey, in the United States and Monte Carlo in Europe, which became famous for their boardwalks, amusement centres and casinos.

The perception of our industrial waterfronts altered significantly in the second half of the 20th century as a response to containerization. As the shipping industry moved the bulk of its activities to the outskirts of cities for economic and logistical imperatives, vast areas of port and port-related buildings and spaces were left abandoned in urban regions worldwide. Marred by toxic waste, these areas quickly fell into disuse and were left abandoned. Artist Gordon Matta-Clark famously explored Manhattan's post-industrial waterfront in the mid-

1970s in works such as "Day's End/Pier 52", in which he cut a crescent-shaped aperture into the wall of a warehouse on a pier at Gansevoort Street. His action opened up unexpected views across the Hudson River and prompted rediscovery of this largely forgotten area of the city.

The outlook of cities changed significantly in the latter part of the century. No longer driven by its industrial heritage, the social and cultural life of the city was instead fuelled by a new service-oriented economy. In response, the waterfront was rediscovered as a potential site for new residential, cultural and recreational developments anchored by the experience of being by the water, offering a combination of urban and rural qualities, as it were. As Ann Breen and Dick Rigby, co-founders of the Waterfront Center in Washington, DC, assert, urban waterfront planning and development became a "civic interest that is persuasive and powerful."[4] Large-scale renewal projects along the waterfronts of various US-American cities such as the Inner Harbor of Baltimore, begun in the 1960s; Seattle port area, undergoing revitalization since the 1970s; the downtown waterfront of Boston, under development since the mid-1980s; and the Embarcadero in San Francisco, which was transformed following the removal of the Embarcadero Freeway, in 1991, destroyed during the Loma Prieta earthquake of 1989. These large-scale initiatives with recreational, commercial, cultural and residential venues providing new live, work, and play spaces became models for other cities. Today, new waterfront developments have come to define urban renewal projects in cities as diverse as Barcelona, Shanghai, Tokyo, Seoul, Yokohama, Liverpool, Valencia, Belfast, Dublin, Bristol, Buenos Aires, Kobe, Rijeka, Split, St. Petersburg, Djakarta, Cape Town, Amsterdam, London, Manila and Osaka.

Millennium Bridge, London, Great Britain, Foster + Partners, Arup and Sir Anthony Caro, 2000. The pedestrian bridge connects the north and south banks of the river Thames between St. Paul's Cathedral and Tate Modern.

Tate Modern, London, Herzog & de Meuron, 2000.

Architecture in Coney Island, Brooklyn, New York, USA. From 1829 on, Coney Island became a beach resort for well-to-do city dwellers.

In the latter half of the 1990s, signature architecture, whether the adaptive re-use of former industrial buildings or innovative contemporary designs inserted into the urban frame as in the case of the Guggenheim Museum in Bilbao became popular signs and symbols of urban redevelopment. Frank Gehry's acclaimed Bilbao Guggenheim, which opened in 1997, became the linchpin in the city's area-wide revitalization. Elsewhere, projects such as Tate Modern in London by Herzog & de Meuron on the South Bank of the Thames illustrate the potential for new architecture to transform the city's edge, encouraging interaction between the city and its waterfront, and providing fresh icons with which to identity and interpret city life.

In other areas of the world, artificially constructed landscapes have inspired unprecedented relationships with water. As landscape architect Adriaan Geuze has pointed out: "Something new is that sand is being sprouted in pancake layers to form land on an extensive scale."[5] He emphasizes leading examples in areas of Asia and the Persian Gulf. In the United Arab Emirates entire cityscapes are being developed on artificial islands that will span approximately 100 square kilometres in total. The Palm Jumeirah, the Palm Jebel Ali and the Palm Deira Islands, for example, off the coast of Dubai are the largest land reclamation projects in the world and will result in the world's largest artificial islands with more than 2,500 properties located on each. Commissioned by Sheikh Mohammed bin Rashid Al Maktoum in an effort to increase Dubai's tourism and population, the projects are part of an overriding plan for Dubai as a residential, leisure, recreational, business and commercial centre. The possibilities appear endless for new developments. However, critics call attention to the challenge to create architectural responses that are ecologically and environmentally

Gordon Matta-Clark, installation "Day's End/Pier 52" (exterior with ice), 1975.

sustainable and that respond to current social and political situations, ensuring their longevity beyond their rapid construction. The world waits in anticipation for the completion of these ambitious schemes; their long-term viability and ecological soundness is yet to be assessed.

Although the nature of the waterfront provides a unique realm for development, entailing social, recreational and environmental benefits as well as serving political and economic interests, the potential for synergy between the built environment and water is not something achieved through a simplistic approach, but a complex and integrated process, requiring mindful strategies, a substantial investment of time, money and above all research and design development. Once determined, however, it also calls for continuous reassessment.

Flood Threats and Responses

As recent history has reminded us, our natural weather systems make clear the dramatic reality of living with water, whether there is too much or too little of that precious resource. The threat of rapidly melting glaciers and the extreme droughts in many parts of the world emphasize the intrinsic relationship between water and the built environment, as do natural disasters as diverse as the flooding in Mozambique due to heavy rains in January 2008; the series of tsunamis triggered in 2004 by an earthquake off the coast of Sumatra, Indonesia that killed more than 225,000 people in eleven countries; and the severe destruction and human tragedy that was the result of Hurricane Katrina when the levees burst in Louisiana causing extensive flooding along the Gulf Coast of the United States in August 2005.

These examples are just some of the recent disasters that accentuate the manifold connections between water and the built environment. Architects, designers and associated professionals worldwide are responding to these threats in their design work. This work has been the centrepiece of numerous biennales, expositions and conferences centred on the topic of water.[6]

In 2008, the US-based History Channel ran a competition for the "City of the Future", and invited architects to submit proposals for what cities might look like 100 years from now. Architecture Research Office from New York presented perhaps the bleakest outlook, proposing that in 2106 intense flooding due to rising sea levels caused by the loss of the earth's polar ice caps will make some of our most familiar urban conurbations unrecognizable. They foresee Manhattan transformed by a new grid of live, work and play spaces built above ground and powered by solar energy that will weave in and out of existing skyscrapers, replacing the existing streetscape that will lie deep under water.

No less critical was the scheme from Chicago-based UrbanLab, an architecture and urban design office, which looked at the potential scarcity of our natural water resources due to increased demands. Sarah Dunn and Martin Felsen, the studio's founders, developed plans for a new water system for their hometown that sets an example of water re-use for the world. They envision a self-contained system that draws water from Lake Michigan, disperses it for use through "Eco-Boulevards" and then returns it to its source via a natural treatment system. The duo note that the Eco-Boulevards will function as "green infrastructure", "cleaning and carrying water" but also housing

The Palm Islands are artificial islands in United Arab Emirates, on which commercial and residential buildings are currently being constructed.

In 2008, Mozambique suffered severe flooding, displacing some 100,000 people.

Hurricane Katrina which hit the Gulf Coast in 2005, was one of the costliest and deadliest hurricanes in United States history, causing damage to thousands of properties and destroying major infrastructure.

Flood conditions during the aftermath of Hurricane Katrina. The most severe loss of life and property damage occurred in New Orleans, Louisiana, which flooded due to failure of the levee system.

Architecture Research Office's proposal for the "City of the Future" focused on inserting a series of "vanes" or new types of mixed-use buildings into Manhattan, replacing the existing streetscape, which they predict will eventually lie deep under water. Luminescent evaporation towers located around the periphery of the city would be used to refine enough water to meet all of the city's needs.

A detail view of the interconnected "vane" system of new buildings. The project proposed that the skin or membrane structure covering the multi-level buildings could collect solar energy to supply power and could be opened to the wind to ventilate individual units or whole corridors.

	Lake
	Existing parks
	Development
	Brownfields
	Eco-Boulevard
	Eco-Buildings
----	Transit

Diagrammatic plans (top 2030, bottom 2060) of a system of Eco-Boulevards, a concept for Chicago by UrbanLab, 2008. Open green space spread throughout the city stitches together historic ethnic and economic boundaries and creates gathering and play spaces as well as community gardens.

"diverse landscape elements including wetlands, prairies, walk/bike trails, open green space, recreation space, marshes, gardens, farms, etc." The proposal places the environmental and ecological imperatives of the built environment at the forefront of new water-related schemes, in addition to the social and cultural life of the city. UrbanLab are currently developing their scheme as part of a region-wide initiative spearheaded by the City of Chicago.

What has become clear is that man's impact on the environment from continuous development and industrial waste has had enormous negative effects, resulting in a landscape too taxed to heal in times of environmental disaster. Following the 2004 tsunami in the Indian Ocean, for example, researchers concluded that areas lined with coastal forests, especially mangroves, were less damaged by the severe weather conditions than areas not buffered by this naturally grown vegetation. Studies conducted by the M.S. Swaminathan Foundation in Chennai, India, conclude that in the five countries most affected by the tsunami – Indonesia, Sri Lanka, India, Thailand and the Maldives – human activities had reduced the area of mangroves by 26 percent between 1980 and 2000. The study also reveals that mangroves, in addition to protecting areas from severe weather and erosion, entail benefits such as enhanced fishing and forestry production that manmade fortifications do not provide.[7]

Neil Burgess, a conservation specialist working with the World Wildlife Fund, draws a correlation between "the degradation of the wetlands in Louisiana", which he asserts "almost certainly increased Hurricane Katrina's destructive powers" and the destruction of mangroves in countries such as India.[8]

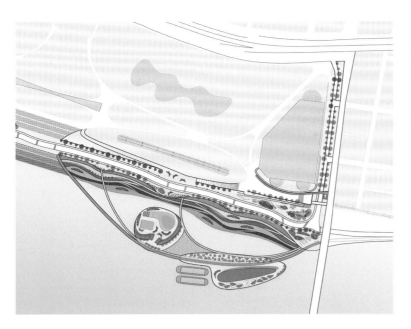

Plan view of a concept by Diana Balmori, 2008, for a new terraced river edge, floating walkways and floating islands that will allow for inhabitation of the Mississippi River and provide greater connections between St. Louis, Missouri, USA, and its waterfront as part of new redevelopment plans for the city.

Diana Balmori's proposal for new waterfront development in St. Louis, Missouri, includes a series of sweeping walkways that will ramp over the water to seamlessly connect the islands to the mainland.

The Mississippi River in the New Orleans region is home to the largest port in the nation and one-quarter to one-third of oil and gas used in the nation is either generated or shipped through the north central Gulf. It is estimated that since the 1930s, 4,000 square kilometres of wetlands have been lost and another 4,000 square kilometres could be lost in the next 40 years, increasing the risk of innumerable damage in the future. In response, this highly trafficked section of the Mississippi is the focus of numerous studies aimed at restoring the area's depleted marshland, due to coastal erosion and poisonous chemical run-off from heavy oil and gas industries, as a natural wall of defense to reduce future hurricane risks.

Diana Balmori, a landscape architect engaged in projects along the Mississippi River, notes that historically, the "issue of water has been fraught with issues of control." She is currently working on developing alternative approaches that work with water rather than against it. "We want to re-envision treatments for our water's edges and introduce new rational and philosophical bodies of thought based on different ways of working with water that can help diminish the damage done by the force of water during adverse weather conditions, as well provide new opportunities for engaging with water."

Balmori calls for a rethinking of the waterfront, "beyond the picturesque."[9] Her New York-based studio is radically redefining the practice of building on water with a heightened sensitivity to the flows of this natural resource. Currently working in St. Louis on a scheme to forge greater connections between a site in front of Eero Saarinen's St. Louis Arch, the city of St. Louis, and the Mississippi River, her team is tackling the the landscape as if it were architecture through built structures in

the form of floating islands, tethered to the land, that rise and fall with the changing height of the level of the water. Outfitted with facilities for boating and ice-skating, and other activities such as dining, the islands are designed with devices meant to specifically address Mississippi currents and cycles. At high water levels, the floating islands are accessible via pontoon walkways, while others are planned so they can be submerged with water. When the river levels drop, the walkways come to rest at ground level, ensuring connections between the islands and riverfront are preserved. Balmori credits the system with making use of "the dynamism of the shifting water levels."[10] In addition, she notes the use of new technologies: working with the naval architecture firm of Consulmar, for example, they developed a structure made from triangular-shaped framework with pockets that can hold vegetation, which can support and shelter aquatic plants, in turn helping to clean the water and providing protected areas for river-life.

Current plans for the New York-New Jersey Upper Bay, an area spanning the entire New York City waterfront from lower Manhattan to the northern reaches on both the east and west sides of the city, also include the creation of a resilient coastline with an archipelago of islands and reefs, tidal marshes, and parks. An interdisciplinary team led by structural engineer Guy Nordenson, a professor at Princeton University, that includes New York-based Architecture Research Office and Catherine Seavitt Studio, is currently working on research for the New York-New Jersey Upper Bay, funded by the Fellows of the American Institute of Architects' Latrobe Prize. The complex coastline of the Upper Bay is laden with challenges based on changes in climate, as well as evolving social and environmental patterns, stemming from the transformation of this once

A proposal for the New York-New Jersey Upper Bay in New York, USA, by a team led by Guy Nordenson aims to transform this area of formerly industrial coastline into living and recreational space. The manifold approach includes the creation of islands in the Upper Bay made from landfill with tidal marshes, piers, parks and new building developments.

An aerial view of the proposed plan for the New York-New Jersey Upper Bay. The design was structured around creating an environment that could evolve over time, addressing changing ecological, technical and economic issues.

industrial waterfront to more recreational use. At the crux of their extensive strategy is the city's evolving relationship with water, given the rapid rise in sea levels, which they predict will dramatically impact local infrastructures, ecosystems and coastal communities by 2050. Rather than proposing traditional engineering fortifications such as seawalls and bulkheads, the team envisions a more flexible approach that includes: the creation of islands in the Upper Bay made from landfills created from excavated matter dredged from the bottom of the bay, a coastline that combines tidal marshes, piers, parks and new developments; and finally a new zoning procedure that would allow for public-private partnerships to be formed to drive the developments, which could evolve over time in response to changing needs, whether environmental, social or cultural. Ultimately, the team's strategy, mapped out in a 400-page document, is conceived as a flexible yet comprehensive vision that not only addresses individual environmental, technical and economic aspects but is driven by a desire to enhance the overall quality of life of the city. In keeping with contemporary thinking and practice, the team's "soft approach" is based on layering programmes such as housing and parks or fresh water storage, urban farms and wetland aquaculture. It aims to not only manage existing conditions but encourage new developments as well as support the ecological revitalization of the harbour area. "Ultimately, we envision the Upper Bay as a new regional centre", says ARO principal Adam Yarinsky. "The concept combines nature, commerce, culture and recreation into a kind of Central Park of the 21st century."[11]

Architect Stanley Allen, an advisor for the New York-New Jersey Upper Bay project and Dean of the School of Architecture at Princeton University, is also engaged in several waterfront projects that aim to resolve issues of flood protection. These include a scheme for a 1-kilometre section of Taipei, which faces the river Danshui and is also bordered by the river Keelung. In 2008, Allen's Brooklyn-based studio was invited by the Taipei City government to generate ideas for this waterfront site and an adjacent parking garage. The challenge was to re-connect the site – currently occupied by parking lots and other sub-standard uses – back to the city, and to provide public access to the water at the western terminus of the city's east-west axis. The main hurdle of the project was an existing 8.6-metre flood wall that borders the two river systems in Taipei, and provides the main source of defense against flooding from the river during typhoon season. The volatile condition of this waterfront, which experiences severe weather patterns annually, limits the plant life to native species from the area that can withstand and thrive in these adverse conditions. The river Danshui is host to one of the most important mangrove forests in Taiwan, which has inspired Allen to propose instating a mangrove forest along the stretch of waterfront covered by his project.

After initially conceptualizing a series of proposals to bridge over the land where it is at its highest points, out of the reach of tidal flooding, or over the wall when protection from flooding is required and the wall is needed, with various landscape components, the designers came up with the idea of working with the wall itself: transforming it in section to allow seamless access and reshaping it at the water's edge with a serpentine form that pushes out at certain points, extending the city out to the water, and retracts inwards at other points, drawing the water closer to the land. "By pushing and pulling the wall in and out at various places, we could work with this obstacle, maintaining the equivalent flood protection but developing the

Current site conditions along the waterfront in Taipei showing 8.6-metre-high flood wall that protects the city from adverse weather conditions and rising river levels, but also cuts the riverfront off from the city.

Stan Allen's vision for a reconfigured coastline, renamed Serpentine Crest Park, will maintain areas of the flood wall where necessary and open other areas for public use. Suggested programmatic uses for these sites include look-out points, a sculpture park, a pool, an amphitheatre, a marina, an eco-learning centre and restaurant and café facilities.

Terraced landscaping with mangroves and grassy lawns

Area with look-out points

Hardscapes: tennis courts, public gathering spaces and a seashell park

Mixed-use tower with a bird aviary

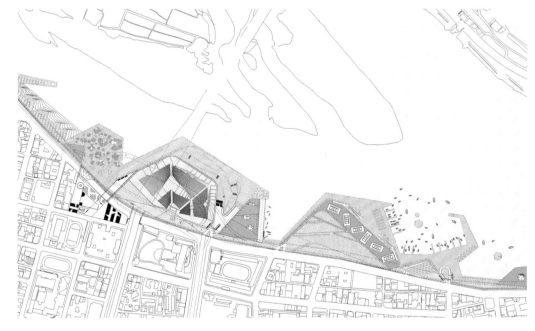

Aerial view of the proposed Serpentine Crest Park looking north, illustrating how the new park will bring the city and the waterfront together. At the centre is a new multi-use tower that will provide both commercial and residential spaces.

A bird's eye view of the planned Treasure Island development, viewed from the new Bay Bridge, which will be completed in 2012. The buildings are equipped with photovoltaic-clad roofs.

Rendering of the envisioned Treasure Island development in San Francisco Bay with the Ferry Building on Market Street in downtown San Francisco in the foreground. Once completed, Treasure Island will be 90 centimetres above the present level of San Francisco's waterfront to account for the rise in sea levels.

landscape at its base in a richer way, and creating an elevated promenade at the crest of the structure that provides views across the city and water", explains Allen.[12] By substantially thickening the width of the wall in parts, the team was able to embed a new parking garage and other programmes within its structure, concealing and distributing these facilities and freeing space for landscape. The insightful design, which was honoured with a Progressive Architecture award from *Architect* magazine in 2009, allows greater areas on the city side to be developed into parks and green space, protected by the wall, as well as new wetlands to be created at the water's edge with indigenous plants that can withstand flooding. A public building situated above the parking garage has also been designated for redevelopment with commercial facilities as well as programming related to the vicinity such as an environmental centre and an aviary. Although Allen notes that the existing wall recalls former Army Corps of Engineers thinking, where the water is to be repelled at all costs, he asserts that, "As we were only working with a small portion of the flood control system, we couldn't change that, but in a small way, both functionally and symbolically, our project offers an alternative. We have embraced the presence of the water, and, through the sloping surfaces and variety of waterfront conditions, we have enhanced the interaction of the city and the river." He concludes: "Our desire was ultimately to work with the water rather than against it."[13]

Water Neutrality

As these projects illustrate, relationships with water are increasingly dominating schemes for new urban developments. Another factor being addressed worldwide is our increasing reliance on healthy ecosystems. While this might seem self-evident, many new architecture and planning projects are still far from where they should be in terms of reducing negative effects on the environment. In the United States, for instance, non-profit groups such as the U.S. Green Building Council and Architecture 2030 make available statistics on the emissions of the building sector and promote changes in the way buildings and developments are planned, designed and constructed, in an effort to dramatically reduce these harmful emissions. Water neutrality, or being able to live within the natural water budget, has become an imperative for projects on waterfront settings. One of the most visionary projects to emerge over the last few years is the ambitious scheme for Treasure Island, a 160-hectare former Naval base just to the north of the San Francisco-Oakland Bay Bridge. The island, currently home for some 1,400 people, is being surveyed by the city in the hope that it can be developed into an ecological urban centre for a population of 13,500 inhabitants. Built on landfill for the Golden Gate International Exposition in 1939, Treasure Island was designated as a naval base during the Second World War. Decommissioned in the late 1990s, it has undergone a series of studies concerning how to preserve and develop it, motivated by growing concerns to make more everyday living conditions more sustainable. "In the past, good design meant mitigating our effects on our environment. Today, it is the reverse", explains Jean Rogers, an environmental engineer with the design and consulting firm Arup, who is working on the Treasure Island project.[14] Envisioning the island as a test site for energy efficiency, renewable energy generation and waste management,

the project places water conservation, preservation and re-use at the centre of a scheme that caters to the entire hydrological cycle. "Climate change, weather patterns and rising sea levels have predicated that we think about the entire life cycle of the island", notes Rogers, whose team is determining amenities for stormwater capture, treatment and reintegration through the use of wetlands constructed on the site, ultimately reducing potable water use by 40 percent, which equates to approximately 270 litres of water used per day rather than 455 litres, the daily average water consumption in the United States. By studying the water cycle, Rogers believes they can begin to mimic natural systems; additional initiatives include on-site treatment and re-use of greywater to meet 100 percent of non-potable water demand. As Rogers asserts, "The vulnerability of Treasure Island, which is subject to climate change, rising sea levels, storms, earthquakes, and hazards from the legacy of contamination that was left on the site, requires an ambitious design to safely reclaim this land. Through sustainable improvements and the implementation of new technologies, our hope is that Treasure Island will once again inspire visitors as a place of innovation."[15]

Chosen for their innovative solutions and high-quality designs, the architectural projects in *Building with Water* – situated on rivers, lakes and at the edges of oceans and seafronts – are visually and physically connected to their sites. In all cases, water provides the impetus for the project. Rather than being treated as ornamental, however, water is the element that determines the design. As these projects attest, the waterfront is becoming the locus of wide-ranging and imaginative redevelopment projects globally. These diverse case studies, ranging from concepts and plans to projects under construction and

recently completed, illustrate the host of motivations – environmental, ecological, social, technological, economic, and ethical – that are driving an increasingly rigorous exploration and set of criteria for new typologies of architecture that engage with water. The projects fall into the categories "Arts and Culture", "Living", "Recreation" and "Industry and Infrastructure", each function with its distinct typology.

The 22 projects discussed in depth range from cultural centres, such as concert halls, museums and performance art venues, that elevate the experience of the waterfront and create a sense of civic pride, to inventive housing solutions such as new concepts for high-rise living, and designs for residences that make previously toxic wastelands habitable through remediation. Commercial facilities that present particularly innovative examples of offices and industrial facilities are also included, as well as recreational venues such as swimming baths and play spaces that provide spectacular meeting places for festivals and community gatherings with panoramic views. These farsighted designs are contemporary reinterpretations of waterfront architecture, creating new destinations with the possibility to touch the water and actively engage with it through recreational and cultural programmes. As the projects illustrate, visionary architecture on both small and large scales can have dramatic impacts on our immediate environment, reframing the landscape and providing new sightlines that encourage rediscovery of familiar places.

The success of these projects, however, is clearly dependent on their relationship to larger redevelopment efforts that go beyond singular acts of architecture and include a commitment to environmental and ecological initiatives, area-wide transportation schemes and the incorporation of a variety of programmes and spaces that can accommodate a diverse array of people. The designs underscore the need for a cohesive approach that focuses on the environmental and ecological aspects but also on achieving outcomes that are politically, economically, educationally and culturally sustainable. Such investments require the commitment of architects, designers, landscape architects, engineers, artists, construction crews and many others, including inspired clients. As Lewis Mumford has stated, "Man cannot achieve a high level of economic life or culture in an environment whose resources he has plundered and defaced. And if even an economic system demands a balance between energy income and outgo, human culture demands a still greater degree of discrimination and care in the use of the environment: a more active sense of place-possibility, a more delicately poised equilibrium between the landscape and the modes of human occupation."[16] As this volume emphasizes, an open-minded approach results in groundbreaking solutions that are responsive to local and wider-scale needs promoting diversity, education, creativity, tolerance and allowing for the exchange of ideas. These compelling designs counter assumptions and introduce new ways of living, working and playing on water.

1 Vandana Shiva, "India and the new Water Wars", *Domus*, no. 905 (July/August 2007), p. 93.

2 Philip Ball, *H₂O: A Biography of Water*, London: Weidenfeld & Nicholson, 1999, p. 121.

3 Charles Moore, *Water and Architecture*, New York: Harry N. Abrams, 1994, p. 23.

4 Ann Breen and Dick Rigby, *The New Waterfront: A Worldwide Urban Success Story*, New York: McGraw-Hill Professional, 1996, p. 27.

5 Adriaan Geuze, *The Flood: 2nd International Architecture Biennale*, Rotterdam: NAi Publishers, 2005, p. 17.

6 In the last few years alone, the Royal Institute of Dutch Architects organized H2olland (2006), an online exhibition about building on water; "The Flood" was the topic of the 2nd International Architecture Biennale in Rotterdam (2007); the Natural History Museum in New York launched the traveling exhibition: H₂O=Life (2007); the International Federation of Landscape Architects selected "Transforming with Water" as the topic of their World Congress (2008), which was also the theme of the 2008 EXPO in Zaragoza, Spain, and the Water Expo in Suzhou, China, of the same year. Water was also the subject of the 2008 Next Generation competition sponsored by *Metropolis* magazine that rewards young architects and designers for sustainable solutions to design problems.

7 www.mssrf.org

8 http://earthobservatory.nasa.gov/Newsroom/view.php?id=28612

9 Based on interviews with Diana Balmori conducted in January 2009.

10 Ibid.

11 Based on email correspondence with ARO conducted in February 2009.

12 Based on interviews conducted with Stanley T. Allen in February 2009.

13 Ibid.

14 Based on interviews with Jean Rogers conducted in January 2009.

15 Ibid.

16 Lewis Mumford, *The Culture of Cities*, New York: Harcourt, Brace and Company, 1938, p. 335.

Where Water Meets the Land:
The Rediscovery of the Waterfront
Dieter Grau | Zeljka Carol Kekez

A highly polluted irrigation canal has been restored as a 1-kilometre-long river which creates an attractive clean waterscape for all generations and a front to the housing estate of Zhiangijawo in Tianjin, China.

The banks are softly moulded and planted, and the water is accessible in many places by boardwalks, steps and ramps.

The world is experiencing an explosion of design and celebration of cultures on the water's edge. Capitalizing on topographical context, cities are commissioning architecturally distinctive landmarks and civic icons to honor interactions with their natural resource, water – the raison d'être for different idiosyncratic urban identities.

From the start, civilizations have flourished, declined and revitalized settlements on rivers, lakes, canals and on the more than 850,000 kilometres of coastline that mark the edges of the world's continents and islands. In early days, the prosperous cradle of a sophisticated civilization, Mesopotamia, located in modern day Iraq and Syria, was situated between the life-giving rivers of Tigris and Euphrates. Also, the ancient societies of Egypt, the Indus Valley and China lived in harmony with life-sustaining and spiritual qualities of water. Small local rivers in Tianjin, China, formerly used for irrigation and farm flooding, now serve as the new waterfront edge for the Zangjiawo residential area. The restored ecological integrity of the river-canal makes it a community asset and a focal point for leisure and socializing for all generations. Throughout the world, cultural history has always been associated with hydrology. The science of aquaculture was also elemental to early societies in South America and in the Mexico Valley where the floating market gardens, *chinampas*, at the remains of the ancient Lake Xochimilco, are still in use. The man-made islands consisting of large planted rafts between the networks of canals allow for harvesting throughout the year. Historically, there is a long tradition of using water as a sculptural element and object of reverence, an inspiration for creativity, defense, art, agriculture and tourism; at the same time, water power has been harnessed for many centuries for entrepreneurial activities.

In the process of settlement, cities such as Venice, Amsterdam, Suzhou and Birmingham thrived on the technology of artificial waterways used for trade, transportation and industry. The mercantile cities of London, Paris, New York, Buenos Aires and Shanghai continue to be lively destinations celebrated for vibrant industrial and civic waterfront identities. Since the late 1980s, the river Thames provided the main impetus for developing the Paddington Basin, The Docklands and the Thames Barrier Park, regenerating some of the most deprived parts of the city and attracting high profile capital investors. Anchored by the bustling water's edge, Tokyo, Chicago and Hong Kong also owe their successful legacies to water routes and the resultant expansion of waterfront commerce, recreation and cultural activities. Renowned for its Victoria Harbour skyline, Hong Kong attracts people to the waterfront, by maritime approach as much as by land, while the Lake Michigan, along with the Chicago and Calumet Rivers, provides a dynamic network of water infrastructure contributing to Chicago's evolving identity. In a similar fashion, Honshū Island, Tokyo Bay and the Pacific Ocean distinguish Tokyo's waterfront as the premier intersection of natural and built environment.

Creating a compelling reinterpretation of the water's edge, islands like Singapore and Stockholm have flourished as thriving waterfront locations. They offer world-class cultural, commercial, recreational and residential amenities near water and encourage ecological exploration of this precious natural resource. In the case of Stockholm, intrinsic natural resources such as the Stockholm Archipelago, Lake Mälaren, the Baltic Sea and the Riddarfjärden Bay offer a strong sense of place for the waterfront itself, blurring boundaries between water and built environment. Looking back in history shows that the im-

The extension of the Dubai Creek forms the edge of the Dubai Business Park Development and creates a high potential for activating the waterfront and implementing a design which increases the outdoor comfort for the people.

portance of water to a society has not changed much. Working in concert with nature to emphasize the cycle of life was an inherent and practical matter for our predecessors. Today, water is not only essential for life, it is imperative to mimic its natural systems to reintegrate waterfront improvements into the surrounding urban fabric as socially and ecologically responsible developments.

In one of the greatest human migrations of modern times, people are rediscovering coastlines around the world, particularly those in Asia and Africa. In the 1950s, New York City was the planet's only megacity. Today, there are 14 coastline megacities with more than 10 million inhabitants, while two-fifths of the world's major cities are located near water.[1] Significantly, future population growth patterns are intensely focused on urban waterfronts of less economically developed countries. In areas of North Africa and the Middle East where access to safe drinking water is scarce, waterfront vitality is continually challenged by social deprivation and physical dereliction. Resuscitating the river Fez in Morocco is an example of a rehabilitation effort combining practical solutions for infrastructure, social, economic and environmental concerns at the water's edge. The goal is to enhance regional water quality while addressing the lack of open public space, overpopulation and an aging infrastructure within the Medina of Fez, the historic city.

The project consists of critical interventions strategically phased to enhance water quality, remediate contaminated sites, create open spaces, and build on existing resources for economic development. According to the Régie Autonome Distribution d'Eau & Électricité de Fés (RADEEF), the Department of Water and Power of the Municipality of Fez, "The

overall effect is a master plan that elevates the river into an urban infrastructure for bridging the gap between the needs of a 21st-century population and the historical standards for preserving the integrity of a UNESCO World Heritage designation."[2]

The successful transformation of Fez and other waterfront efforts worldwide depends on a dynamic and farsighted vision, flexible implementation plans and a commitment to sustainable initiatives. In the case of Dubai, the world's fastest growing city – at least until a recent economic bust – the waterfront is home to ambitious designs for some of the world's largest artificial islands. Though impressive in scale and imagination, these illustrious land reclamation efforts present a challenge for the health of the Persian Gulf. Though environmentalists speculate of their potential to cause profound ecological transformations, only time will reveal true lessons and set the stage for new expressions of city aspirations.

The 35-hectare Dubai Business Park site located adjacent to the proposed extension of the Dubai Creek lies some 10 kilometres west of the existing Central Business District (CBD) of Dubai and is about 7 kilometres from the airport. The waterfront planning and design for the Business Park and Dubai Creek extension, which attracts people and uses to the water's edge for cultural, recreational and residential developments, was a serious challenge considering harsh local climatic conditions. In an effort to offer a counter example to the big palm island projects, Atelier Dreiseitl, a planning office for water schemes based in Überlingen, Germany, collaborated, from the inception of the project, with ecological specialists applying sustainable design approaches to generate a clean and healthy

Portland, Oregon, served as the timber and grain export gateway to Asia but its port industry went into decline after the 1950s.

In 1927, the city built a seawall of some 10 metres height to protect its urban core from unpredictable water level fluctuations. Today, the wall is deteriorating and hinders access to the water.

waterscape at the water's edge. As the Dubai Creek already faces water quality problems, the concept was based on tidal energy without the use of pumps.

Envisioned as a place for pedestrian and bicycle experience, the promenade offers opportunities for enjoying nature, people-watching and active recreation. Cafés and ice cream parlours are situated along the water's edge on the way to the Seaside Plaza. The promenade is staged in different levels stepping down to the waterfront adorned with an artistic paving pattern of a unique character. The Seaside Plaza is partially sheltered by trees and shading structures with a stage for public events. Highlighted through a series of water features, ending with a cascade into the creek, the plaza creates a refreshing atmosphere and emphasizes the visual axis with the Central Business District.

To optimize public use, large-scale waterfront master plans such as the Dubai waterfront should have appropriate phasing implementation steps. Often unveiled with the promise of recapturing land that has fallen into disrepair, large-scale waterfront master plans are difficult to implement and parts often never get built. The same excitement that captures the public's imagination and the media's attention for these mega plans can also bring about their demise. It is therefore crucial to have strong community outreach garnering broad public support.

Throughout history, similar experimental and thought-provoking urban development near the water's edge led to comparable patterns of environmental use. Many waterfronts were left decrepit and disconnected from neighbouring communities. Important wetland habitats, coral reefs, rivers and estuaries

were being degraded or destroyed. Struggling with conflicting agendas, generations of government leaders have mismanaged long-term waterfront visions producing only mediocre results. That's why in recent times, designers, engineers and municipal leaders have often been criticized for focusing solely on iconic waterfront projects occupying the land adjacent to the waterfront rather than on a holistic waterfront experience embracing a delicate balance of the natural and built environment.

The Succession of Waterfront Uses

Water and waterfront activities have always been strategic resources in the world, a symbol of life, and impetus for development of human settlements. Since the beginning, as engines of economic growth, cities have subscribed to evolving technologies to alter the shape and the pace of their waterfront redevelopment efforts. Many coastal communities owe their origin and prosperity to access to water, successful cultivation of land near the water's edge, related craftsmanship, industry and trade as well as water transport.

Initially, industrial ports were gateway destinations where the movement and exchange of goods were facilitated and urban services developed to promote maritime trade. Subsequently, a waterfront served as the focal point of activity, the place where water-related and urban-based functions merged. Anchoring liquid highways of worldwide commerce that carried people and goods from the heartlands to the coasts and then across the oceans, the waterfronts of the world adapted to everchanging needs of a growing urban population.

Barcelona established one of the most recognized urban waterfront redevelopments of the 20th century. Urban beaches, parks and an emphasis on outstanding design contributed to its success. Triggered by the Olympics in 1992, the Port Vell, the city's old obsolete and run-down harbour, was transformed into a popular urban area featuring an entertainment complex and a large aquarium, next to the old customs building Aduana from 1902.

These swimming facilities on the waterfront, designed by Beth Galí in 2004, are part of the Barcelona Forum.

Along the Columbia and Willamette Rivers in the Pacific Northwest, Portland, Oregon, USA, served as the timber and grain export gateway to Asia and the gold fields of California in the 19th century. Similar to other premier freshwater ports around the world, Portland has had its challenges in sustaining its harbour's competitive standing and waterfront vitality. The accumulation of industrial waste and raw sewage, frequent flooding and pollution, had forced businesses to locate away from the waterfront. Portland was not unique in its decline of port industry and its effort of constructing a seawall, built in 1927 and approximately 10 metres tall, to separate downtown businesses from the unhealthy waters and to protect its urban core from unpredictable water level fluctuations. Capitulating to the rise of automobile and presence of national interstates along its banks, further hindered Portland's access to its waterfront as recently as in the 1970s. Since then, Portland's River Renaissance programme has been focused on a long-term vision and a layered approach to waterfront development efforts. The strategy of linking Portland's diverse neighbourhoods and districts back to the rivers aided the city in creation of a dynamic waterfront skyline.

Previously predominantly industrial and then imbued with romanticism through the passage of time, waterfronts continue to be visually seductive settings and one of the main attractions in a city. They certainly should not be places to pass through in a car cutting people off from a distinctive public asset and opportunities for enjoyment, leisure and recreation. Many great cities throughout the world including New York, Seattle, Barcelona and Paris, share a history of subordinating panoramic views to a drive-by experience. It was and still is not uncommon to encounter raised freeways, levees and parking lots dominating stunning waterfront views.

The Alaskan Way Viaduct in Seattle is a double-decked elevated highway that carries up to 110,000 vehicles per day. It continues to represent a barrier between Puget Sound, downtown and the waterfront.

Barcelona's old waterfront on the Mediterranean was much like those of many US cities such as Portland or Philadelphia on the Delaware: the area by the water was taken up by industrial land no longer in use and cut off from pedestrians by a highway. However, Mayor Pasqual Maragall changed the face of Barcelona's shores in his 15 years as mayor from 1982 to 1997. Growth in the city was once focused away from the waterfront, exemplified by the placement of its highway near the water, separated from the rest of Barcelona and making it a polluted site. However, local officials had the insight to approach their Olympics plan as a major restructuring of the city. The high-profile nature of the Games expanded the possibilities for transformation and urban improvements. The city's plan for the 1992 Olympic Games put the highway underground, thus reconnecting the city with its waterfront. Maragall used the money the Games brought to reshape the city's form by forging an open, well-defined relationship to the sea. On this newly open land, he fashioned new beaches, parks and housing neighbourhoods.

Port Vell connects to the Rambla, Barcelona's central pedestrian axis, via a pedestrian bridge that crosses a marina. Further east is Olympic Village, a new neighbourhood mix of public and private housing built from scratch: once the housing for athletes, it is now a new piece of the city. Integrating Olympic Village into the Barcelona fabric required reconstructing the highway so that it now ran underground, an arduous reorganization of railroad, sewage and water infrastructure that proved incredibly valuable.

Seattle's Alaskan Way Viaduct also continues to represent a barrier between Puget Sound, downtown and the waterfront.

To mitigate the waterfront's automobile dominance, Seattle spent more than a decade in planning. It managed to secure nearly 7 hectares of contiguous waterfront property and bring them into public ownership. An extensive series of public meetings and development ideas resulted in a central waterfront revitalization design that melded traditional waterfront uses with the tools of modern international trade. The central waterfront is now a prime example of how judicious real estate development can bolster an area's economic health by attracting local residents as well as tourists and adding to the city's cultural vitality through its mixed uses and interests.

In Bogotá, Colombia, Enrique Peñalosa, the former mayor from 1998 until 2001, resisted the accepted wisdom that more highways and roads for cars would bring economic health to his city. Instead, he rejected a plan to build an elevated beltway around Bogotá and instead spent the money on paved bikeways, sports facilities and parks. Since leaving office, Peñalosa has been travelling the world, sharing his philosophy with cities like Djakarta, Dar Es Salaam, Mexico City, New York and San Francisco.

San Francisco's shoreline on the bay was one of the busiest areas of foot traffic in the world in the early 20th century. However, following the construction of the Bay Bridge and the decline of ferries, the area fell into decline. The rise of the automobile led to the Embarcadero Freeway being built in the 1960s, improving auto access to San Francisco but dividing the waterfront from downtown. Yet, the combination of the 1989 Loma Prieta earthquake and community opposition led to a total transformation of the shoreline and the creation of one of the most dynamic waterfronts in the United States.

The Magellan-Terrassen, designed by Benedetta Tagliabue and
Enric Miralles, are an urban plaza in the HafenCity development.
They opened in 2005 and provide a transition from the city to
the water.

The new urbanist and smart growth development on the waterfront of the San Francisco Bay Area incorporates programming
of the series of waterfront destinations such as the city of Hercules, a company town founded in the late 19th century some
30 kilometres north-east of San Francisco and recently the site
of several redevelopment efforts. The town is undergoing a
metamorphosis into a transit-oriented mixed-use destination.
Its Bayfront plan for 17 hectares of waterfront commercial land
demonstrates how important it is to complement 4.5 hectares
of open space with a density and mix of uses. The Bayfront
will also include an intermodal transit centre with an Amtrak
railway station and a ferry terminal connecting Hercules with
downtown San Francisco. When fully built out, Bayfront is supposed to have 1,224 residential units, 3,900 square metres of
retail space, 7,525 square metres of offices and 12,450 square
metres of flex space adaptable for a variety of uses.

Commercial and residential developments in San Francisco and
surrounding urban communities play an important role in forming a lively waterfront integrated with a range of public uses.
Domination of waterfront sites by single use development such
as housing, green space or industry squanders opportunities
for creation of a vibrant waterfront.

Transformations of the waterfronts' functional and spatial conditions were initially triggered by deindustrialization of the port
enterprise and changes in the predominant trade routes. Global
trends in the logistics of water transportation became apparent
by the 1950s,[3] but it was not until the later 1960s that the prob-
lem of waterfront deterioration and the demand for revitalization policies achieved widespread recognition. The decline of
ship building and its relocation from Europe and North America
to other regions of the world in the 1970s and 1980s, especially
to Australasia where labour costs were lower, also contributed
to the decline of many ports. The profound restructuring of
the global trade, emergence of a new international geography
and increased environmental regulations signaled a remarkable
change in the economic vitality of waterfronts worldwide.

Innovation in global logistics and standardization of ship
cargo further altered the functional and spatial configuration
of world's waterfronts. Today, 26 percent of all containers
originate from China, while 85 percent of the world's goods,
services and capital investments are exchanged between the
economically most powerful regions of Western Europe, North
America and Asia. To relieve heavy congestion of transportation activities in urban areas, port facilities were relocated
and cities were left with degraded sites often triggering programmes of urban renewal. One such example that vividly
illustrates the separation of port and urban functions during
the second half of the 20th century is the City of Hamburg.

The traditional harbour basins and riverside quays next to the
Hamburg city centre continue to be used for conventional shipping and in recent times, goods storage. Without affecting the
economic interests of the port, the City of Hamburg recovered
the area for expansion of the city centre. When the project of
HafenCity was formally established by the City Parliament Act
of August 1997, Hamburg returned to the river Elbe after more
than 100 years. Located on a 157-hectare site, HafenCity is one
of the most prominent city centre development projects in Europe and will increase the size of Hamburg's city centre by 40
percent. Situated directly between the historic Speicherstadt
warehouse district and the river Elbe, a new city will be com-

HafenCity with its central location and a size of 157 hectares is one of the most prominent urban development projects in Europe and will increase the size of Hamburg's city centre by 40 percent.

1 Elbe Philharmonic Hall   3 Site for proposed Science Centre
2 Magellan-Terrassen   4 International Maritime Museum

prised of a cosmopolitan mix of apartments, service businesses, culture, leisure, tourism and retail. An early competition won by KCAP proposed a mixed-use vibrant harbour development with strict ecological stewardship. The development of the entire area is anticipated to continue until 2020–2025.

In the context of worldwide economic restructuring, substitute in dock labour and the urban spatial framework of city and port, Hamburg and other cities worldwide struggle with abilities to accommodate changes and remain viable nodes in a global trade network. Modifications in the pattern of passenger transportation, importance of and challenges inherent in waterfront zoning and land use regulations, environmental policy, development incentives, community participation and public-private partnership have all contributed to the abandonment of traditional urban waterfronts and assisted in an evolution of its new identity.

The succession of different waterfront uses throughout the ages explains the connection between land use during urbanization efforts and current-day environmental degradation. Today's visible evidence of dilapidation in harbours represents an accumulation of effects over several hundred years of intensive developmental periods – agricultural, exploration and trade, industrial and urban renewal and renaissance. Ongoing environmental activists' efforts and media presentation of images of dead fish, oiled birds and flaming rivers support sustainable initiatives claiming that all is not right in a world driven by rapid industrialization, global competition and speculative land development.

Especially in the current situation of economic bust, evolving physical, social and environmental patterns and contributing factors of climate change, the access to clean water and sanitation services is vital for survival and healthy life. The popularity and necessity of living by the water's edge still remains a fundamental catalyst for re-discovery of the world's waterfronts as attractive locations to live, work and play.

The city of Vancouver, British Columbia, surrounded by the waters of the Burrard Inlet, the Fraser River and False Creek, has recently transitioned from a primary port city to a place of consistent economic growth. Central to the rebirth of Vancouver's downtown lifestyle, the False Creek area is a model for defining Vancouver's identity and revitalization success. The entire False Creek waterfront is united by the Seawalk, a recreational trail that maintains public access to the water at all points. Infusing a dynamic combination of activity and life into residential neighbourhoods while building connections with the University of British Columbia and to the Olympic Village, the Seawalk has been crucial to the success of False Creek's rise to a premier urban community. It demonstrates that waterfront redevelopment projects adjacent to downtown areas can succeed if they are well-planned, make the best use of the existing assets of the site, and have a sustained vision for long-term implementation.

"On the opposite side of the False Creek is Granville Island, an industrial reclamation and redevelopment project acclaimed as a highly successful public space. The city transformed this brownfield industrial site into a mixed-use development with residences, artist studios, light industry, a marina and a vast marketplace complete with a farmer's market, a brewery, restaurants and indoor and outdoor public space. The success that

Aker Brygge in Oslo, a former shipyard, has been redeveloped into a lively and densely packed mixed-use district.

The new quarter features a public promenade by the water, offering views of Oslo Fjord.

is Granville Island represents a long-range joint planning strategy of the Canadian federal government and the City of Vancouver in the 1970s. The Granville Island Trust was founded in 1976 to manage the project, improving the physical space with walkways, roads and play areas. Then artists' studios and retail began to fill the space, and today it is a magnet both for tourists and Vancouver's inhabitants."[4] Vancouver – but also Porto and Copenhagen – are just some of the examples that rate as premier urban destinations with a poetic balance of temporary and permanent waterfront activities for all habitats and generations, year-around.

Renaissance of Waterfront Development

Port cities are among the oldest and most advantageous urban settlements. As gateways to the world and centres of commerce in the early 20th century, waterfronts of the past were susceptible to abandonment due to a single-use function. Over several centuries, waterfronts have experienced complex patterns of growth and decline, yielding a substantial urban heritage. In the 1990s, progressive industrial ports began to garner public enthusiasm to initiate mixed-use and green approaches to waterfront redevelopment. Focusing on water as the determining design element, contemporary planning efforts, such as those in Oslo, seek to promote conservation, preservation and re-use of this precious natural resource.

Aker Brygge, a former shipyard shut down in 1982 and located at the Oslo Fjord, is an area in the City of Oslo close to the remarkable City Hall from 1950. Now a vibrant and densely packed mixed-use district with its public promenade, it offers an attractive public space. Amenities include protection from inclement weather and an area for strolling that has become the

focal point of the harbour and the entire city of Oslo. Tourists and locals enjoy the cafés, playgrounds, sittable steps, engaging public art, floating restaurants and small fishing boats that sell their catch at the dock. A few old industrial buildings were demolished, while several of the major workshop halls were rebuilt as retail shops.

Water's edges continue to provide a natural setting for memorable urban destinations. Presenting unparalleled opportunities for spaces that can accommodate diverse programmes, uses and people, the renewed planning energy has been focused on mixed-use waterfront communities. Respecting urban context and the ecological integrity of its watershed, waterfronts around the globe are experiencing urban renaissance and are now being revived as political, economic, educational and cultural centres.

A fusion of ground-breaking sustainable solutions also notably serves to obtain funding for waterfront redevelopment. Havana, Cuba; Santos, Brazil; Mumbai, India; and Dalian, China are among examples that illustrate the process of renewed commitment to improvements of water quality, reduction of noise and visual pollution, habitat restoration and green building practices.

Ecological restoration and structural and spatial improvements involve high costs, progress is normally slow and returns on investments are not immediate, but, as Zanzibar illustrates, a new spirit of revival is broad and international financial aid is available. There is also an increasing awareness, both local and global, of the need to conserve elements of urban architectural heritage that are frequently in danger of being lost. Significantly, a need exists to conserve and enhance the distinctiveness of urban, especially waterfront environments in developing countries, considering that revitalized waterfronts in advanced countries have often acquired an unwelcome similarity in their search for mixed-use renewal. Fostering public-private partnerships in the context of long-range, comprehensive planning and development efforts, urban waterfronts seek to enhance links with the city centre.

The popularity of living, playing and working by the waterfront is evident through a creative interface between waterfront redevelopment and architectural place-making. Large investments are being planned to have major influences on the form of cities – as spaces of promise. Some of the most attractive public spaces with unique character are Coney Island, New York City, Paris Rive Gauche, the area around the London Eye as well as Rome with the new Maxxi National Modern Art Museum on the river Tiber by Zaha Hadid which opened in 2010. Celebrated architectural icons like this one are regularly commissioned to generate an exciting waterfront experience with credibility and public enthusiasm for rediscovery. Another waterfront masterpiece by Zaha Hadid in Italy was envisioned to rejuvenate and regenerate the water's area. Reggio Calabria, located on the Strait of Messina, decided to invest resources in the beautiful seaside kilometre of the harbour, to create a prestigious project that would become a symbol of the community. The complex, realized with private as well as public funding, will consist of two different buildings; a Museum of Mediterranean History and a multi-functional building for performing arts, with a library, auditoria, gym, craft workshop areas and a cinema. Keeping its connection with the Reggio Calabria area strong, the museum will be dedicated to one of the most

famous people coming from the region, Gianni Versace. With a design drawing inspiration from organic forms and aiming for distinctive shapes to be visible both from the sea and the coast, the complex is set to become one of the region's most contemporary landmarks.

Collaborating with architects of international prominence, world cities like Rome are generating renewed interest and excitement about ambitious designs near the water's edge. However, designers sometimes lose the long-term perspective, paying too much attention to the physical infrastructure and not enough to the surrounding ecosystem, history and cultural heritage. They ignore the social fabric of the communities in the planning process, which frames the water as a public good. Significant criticism was levelled against lifeless architecture in recent times for its inability or unwillingness to deliver on the modernist promise of urban equality.

Some argue that Frank Gehry's acclaimed Bilbao Guggenheim Museum, situated on the river Nervión, a symbol of urban redevelopment, is a short-term and short-sighted solution as a waterfront redevelopment. Specifically disputed as a pure design statement, this bold waterfront icon is perceived as a barrier between the city centre and the river, consuming the prime waterfront real estate and limiting activity of the public space around it. Often, the Bilbao Guggenheim Museum is challenged as an example of private development dampening meaningful community involvement, discouraging public-private partnerships and limiting pedestrian experience to a singular destination.

Still, not every community can pull off what the Guggenheim Museum did. The redevelopment of the Abandoibarra district along the river Nervión has been the target of many of Bilbao's long-term plans, yet to be implemented. The area of about 35 hectares is in a prime location identified as the new centre of the city. In former days, it was a zone dominated by shipyards, a container port facility and a regional rail line. Successful waterfront developments like Bilbao serve as an example of waterfront cities emerging from a comprehensive vision, a living process with a dynamic combination of values, aspirations and economic possibilities narrating a story of forward-thinking citizens.

Principles of Waterfront Planning and Design

In a time of spectacular waterfront highlights, according to Franz-Josef Höing's "Open Spaces for Hamburg's HafenCity", the proposed waterfront structures must weather the ups and downs of the economy as well as the changing trends in architecture.[5] The principle applies not only to Hamburg, but to other global cities undergoing rapid development as well.

Unfortunately, some fast-growing cities around the world, like Ahmedabad, Manila and Panama City are quickly ceding their prime waterfront space to excessive privatization and missing an opportunity of a lifetime to protect public access to and along the urban waterfront. According to the Waterfront Center,[6] the private development is a necessary component of the waterfront renaissance process that should fit within the community's vision, not override it.

Along with enhanced environmental stewardship, waterfronts have a heritage of serving as central places of political, economic, social and cultural interchange. To varying degrees, the hallmark of their successful evolution has been a focus on a clean, safe and active public open space, including ongoing management; maintenance or provision of public access to the water's edge; enhanced continuity rather than increased separation between waterfront urban core and neighbourhoods; the conservation and sensitive development of natural resources; seasonal activities; multi-modal access; the cultivation of a diverse community as well as the preservation of links with the past. Utilizing a combination of these practices, waterfronts have evolved from traditional maritime functions to vital nodes in the exchange of ideas and connectivity in the 21st century. Cities like Barcelona, Beijing and Sydney, chosen to host events of an international prominence, have capitalized on unique opportunities to advance their urban infrastructures and waterfront developments.

Serving as links in a global network and cities' front yards, waterfronts have always been the soul of the city reflecting the community's unique character and local distinctiveness. Recently becoming leading sites for achieving urban transformation, waterfronts compete at a global scale to attract new residents, business and visitors. At present, the land near the water's edge is a shared space embracing highly contrasting views where the perspectives of local communities, developers, politicians, planners, port authorities and environmentalists need to be reconciled. The revitalization of Toronto's waterfront provides the city, the province and the country with an excellent opportunity to ensure that Toronto remains among the best places in the world to live, work and visit. Revitalization is a significant key to future prosperity and Canada's much envied standard of living.

In 2006, the Toronto Central Waterfront Design Competition was launched to redevelop this underused part of the city by Lake Ontario. Promenades, parks and plazas at the water's edge were to be created over a stretch of 3 kilometres.

top left: Visualization

right: Model of pedestrian pier

The competition entry by Foster + Partners / Atelier Dreiseitl proposed to create three pedestrian piers as extensions of main downtown streets, thus linking downtown Toronto and its waterfront.

Following the release of the Toronto Waterfront Revitalization Task Force's report in March 2000, the Government of Canada, the Province of Ontario and the City of Toronto jointly announced their support for the creation of Waterfront Toronto to oversee and lead waterfront renewal. Over 800 hectares of strategically located land in the heart of Canada's economic engine – Toronto's Central Waterfront – were mostly vacant and underused. With about 70 percent of the land already in public hands, the City had an extraordinary opportunity to engineer a seamless renewal and position Toronto for intense urban competition in the new millennium.

The development of similar successful waterfront projects in other cities such as London, New York and Barcelona has shown that a separate corporation with a strong mandate to coordinate and oversee an integrated strategy is crucial to making waterfront revitalization a reality. To put Toronto at the forefront of global cities in the 21st century, the city worked with the community and the public and private sectors transforming the water's edge into parks, public spaces, cultural institutions and diverse and sustainable commercial and residential communities.

Toronto exemplifies one of the principal challenges in promoting a coherent waterfront redevelopment plan, namely the reconciliation of differing perspectives and amalgamation of diverse objectives. Cultivating a sense of ownership and pride, an inclusive public participation process allows for transparency, the involvement of informed citizens and a long-term thriving waterfront community.

Consequently, a viable waterfront plan is more than just a design statement or an economic development plan; it is rather a delicate balance of the overall mix that makes living on the edge an attractive proposition. To offer sustainable qualities of a livable community, a new waterfront development needs to intensely embrace its community values and cultural heritage, its economic niche and its unique natural features and essential character within the greater urban context and global connectivity. As showcase examples for sustainability and new social optimism, vibrant waterfront environments such as Toronto continue to inspire the imagination for future generations.

Though most of the world's great cities boast exciting waterfront settings, they have neglected opportunities to create lively public destinations where people will naturally want to gather. From Barcelona to New York to Hong Kong, cities have both squandered great opportunities to create waterfront experiences and implemented viable waterfront projects. Despite mixed results, waterfronts should not be viewed as economic or environmental burdens; they rather offer enormous opportunities to create new public spaces and rejuvenate old ones.

Waterfront planning and development requires preparing for a future that is often impossible to predict, and so must incorporate uncertainty. Forecasts should usually describe ranges of possibilities. Although the present economic circumstances are likely to impede the completion of some projects, a trend in the conversion of urban waterfront areas should emphasize a mix of uses with residential, cultural and commercial components. Increasingly, the city waterfronts are becoming the locus of the most extensive and imaginative redevelopment projects currently under way in the central city.

An urban beach in the heart of a dense city was the vision for the HTO Park, designed by Janet Rosenberg at the Toronto Waterfront. It opened in 2007.

Often the individual waterfront projects are subject of open architectural competitions; this was also the case for the Toronto Waterfront. In 2006, the Toronto Central Waterfront Design Competition was envisioned as 3-kilometre stretch of promenades, parks and plazas at the water's edge between Bahurst Street and Parliament Street. The design concept of the team Foster+Partners and Atelier Dreiseitl was to bring the city to the water and the water back into the city. The goal was to overcome the separation between downtown Toronto and its waterfront, providing a continuity of space in a pedestrian-oriented experience. The proposed competition scheme comprised a series of three piers extending outward from the heads of slips and mirrored, thus extending back into the city.

The Foster+Partners/Atelier Dreiseitl master plan was founded on a holistic strategy for the city – one that could be realized in phases as funds became available. The overall design concept for Toronto Waterfront reduced stormwater run-off by detaining rain water. Despite some breakthrough ecological design ideas by the Foster+Partners/Atelier Dreiseitl team, the winning proposal for the Central Waterfront Design Competition was delivered by West 8. Focusing on triple bottom line (i.e. an approach striving to reconcile economic, ecological and social success), West 8 submitted a design proposal seeking a sustainable agenda and incorporating economic, social and environmental issues. Since the competition four years ago, the progress on the waterfront includes the new HTO Park designed by Janet Rosenberg as well as the three heads of slips designed by West 8 with variations of undulating pedestrian decks over water. Fostering the historic connection of the city with the water, new segments of the waterfront will be implemented as funding becomes available.

Singapore is an example of a progressive world city striving for a comprehensive approach in future urban planning and design, landscape architecture and sensitive environmental engineering on the water's edge. Not content with being just a Garden City, Singapore is re-imagining the idea of living by its edge while integrating blighted urban landscape with green open space. In the reclamation process, Telok Ayer Basin was removed from the map, while the Singapore River's mouth now flows into the bay instead of directly into the sea. A barrage was completed in 2008 to make Marina Bay a reservoir for drinking water adding 20 percent of the original size or 135 km² as of 2003, with plans for additional 99 km². The downtown waterfront at Marina Bay has been designated to become a lifestyle hub with round-the-clock vibrancy and energy. The plan envisions residential, office and commercial developments, as well as many entertainment outlets and attractions to inject life into the area. The city's evolving relationship with the water is the central idea of a plan embraced and supported by the government. Retaining the deepwater working port close by and integrating waterfront development into the urban fabric of surrounding neighbourhoods has been the key to Singapore's ecologically responsible reorganization of the water's infrastructure.

Moving towards self sufficiency in water resources, Singapore has adopted the strategy of stormwater decentralization: stormwater collection and treatment are no longer concentrated at nature reserves, and will occur on every possible surface that the rain falls on – including dense urban areas accounting for a large percentage of Singapore's land mass. In particular, the Marina Barrage is a significant milestone in efforts to maximize Singapore's rainwater harvesting capacity and create a sustainable water supply. A dam built across the mouth of the

Singapore is an island state without aquifers and with a population of 5 million inhabitants; hence there is the necessity of capturing rainwater for use as drinking water.

Water from the largest and most urbanized catchment area, draining stormwater from approximately one-sixth of Singapore, is now collected in the Marina Reservoir. Moving towards self-sufficiency in water resources, Singapore has adopted the strategy of stormwater decentralization.

The river Kallang in Singapore, currently running in an inaccessible concrete channel, will be renaturalized.

Marina Channel creates Singapore's 15th reservoir and the first water reservoir in the city. "The largest and most urbanized catchment, draining stormwater from approximately one-sixth of Singapore, is now collected in the Marina Reservoir. Singapore is an example of a modern city transforming an attractive and active waterfront while incorporating water infrastructure with access to a clean and essential water resource for the city's freshwater supply needs.

Sparkling rivers with landscaped banks, kayakers paddling in the streams, clean waterways flowing into picturesque lakes – this scenario is a not-so-distant dream for every Singaporean. The city leadership is committed and projects are underway to transform Singapore into a City of Gardens and Water where people love to live, work and play. The Public Utility Board's "Active, Beautiful and Clean (ABC) Waters Programme" is the most strategic initiative undertaken to date to realize this vision on the island. Under the stewardship of PUB, the design team of Atelier Dreiseitl and CH2M HILL is undertaking first implementation steps by renaturalizing the river Kallang based on their compiled master plan for the central watershed of the city.

Key Factors for Successful Waterfront Redevelopment

As memorable destinations, waterfront cities are the convergence point for two intensely complex ecosystems, the natural ecosystem of the water's edge and the built ecosystem of concentrated human settlement. Historically, waterfronts have not been strategically or comprehensively planned and though many share similar characteristics, each waterfront is a reflection of a unique past. Through cycles of boom and bust, waterfronts have become the heart and the soul of a community embodying citizens' aspirations for the quality of life.

Enhancing community values with a desire for global connectivity is one of the central tenets of a successful master plan focusing on the long-term vision. Blurring boundaries between water and the built environment while respecting natural resources is critical to a pleasant experience on the water's edge.

With a commitment to sustainable development, the issues of future concern for the successful waterfronts of the world represent a complex matrix of natural, cultural, social, economic and political factors. As centres of intense redevelopment, newly revitalized seaports and inland waterfronts should denote a distinct sense of place. Linking the downtown centre and surrounding neighbourhoods with the water's edge through multi-modal access remains the key in successful transformation of waterfront cities. Strong government leadership coupled with financial commitment, public-private-partnerships and community participation are necessary process ingredients leading to social improvement of waterfronts. Incorporating an approach of building on existing resources for economic progress, the waterfront redevelopment also needs to maintain and improve the water infrastructure and freshwater supply, as well as sewage and wastewater treatment. Equally significant for the success of a waterfront redevelopment is ensuring amenity values of beaches and waterfront properties while preserving public access and offering a variety of cultural, commercial, recreational, residential and entertainment activities appropriate for all seasons.

Encouraging urban renewal through waterfront and shoreline regeneration is a long-term planning process requiring a flexible implementation plan. Strategically phased waterfront development will prevent or minimize encroachment onto critical natural ecosystems, enhance water quality, create public open space and reduce noise and visual pollution.

Protecting against local flooding and subsidence through continuing engineering works as well as planning for projected sea-level rise, increased storms and saltwater intrusions from climate change are topics that will need to be incorporated into waterfront master plans encouraging emerging bioengineering methods to age-old civic infrastructure problems. Learning from the example of Singapore could mean that the main goal for the future is positioning waterfronts as ongoing catalysts for economic, environmental and social transition of mega cities into a sustainable organism – where natural resources like water contribute to the health of the entire ecosystem.

Living on the Edge

We are certainly living on the edge, not only a physical brink of the built and natural environment near water, but also on the edge of times when our way of life will destroy the balance of the planet. Starting now, we have to concentrate our global efforts on sustainable waterfront planning and ongoing management and maintenance for safe, active and clean public open space near the water's edge. Public officials and architects also have to play a significant role in reinvigorating urban design beyond the recent trend of architectural waterfront icons. Award-winning masterpieces and decorative implementations by the water are certainly helpful for urban identity but do not contribute to long-lasting success and livability of our environment. Future concepts in waterfront planning can only be achieved in a common effort of the design and engineering disciplines in partnership with developers, authorities, stakeholders and the public.

Ultimately, waterfront planning begs an age-old question, namely why is living at the water's edge so appealing to the human race and why is building on water so attractive worldwide? Each waterfront locale creates a distinct environment conveying a set of unique values and inspirations to every individual. Without the water, neither iconic architecture, nor incredible art, nor cutting edge design can achieve such a lively and constantly changing world, increasing the stimulation of our senses and elevating our experience to live in harmony with the natural environment.

1 John Tibbetts, "Coastal Cities: Living on the Edge", *Environmental Health Perspectives*, November 2002.

2 Design to Improve Life! www.indexaward.dk

3 Various factors played a role in the decline of ports: The shift from railroad transportation to trucks (which needed space to maneuver that did not necessarily exist) the development of ever-larger cargo ships that some ports could no longer accommodate, the relocation of heavy industry (which relied on material brought through the port) from inner-city sites to cheaper sub-urban locations and the growing resistance against transportation of heavy goods through the city centre are amongst the changes that eroded the importance of many ports.

4 "Case Study – Vancouver: Granville Island & False Creek" www.PlanPhilly.com

5 Franz-Josef Höing, "Freiräume für die HafenCity Hamburg. Open Spaces for Hamburg's HafenCity". *Topos*, no. 48, 2004. Coastlines and Harbours. www.topos.de/media/Heftthema/b0162665_Franz.pdf

6 The Waterfront Center, a non-profit educational organization, was formed in 1981 in the belief that waterfronts – where the land meets the ocean, bay, lake, river or canal – are unique, finite resources. www.waterfrontcenter.org

Towards Flood-Resilient Urban Environments
Chris Zevenbergen

Monsoon-caused flooding in the city of Fatehpur in Rajasthan, India.

Yesterday's Cities

Many cities around the world are facing the challenges of sustainable living and development and are exploring ways to enhance their ability to manage an uncertain future. In the developing world these challenges are often due to increasing concentrations of vulnerable people in vulnerable locations adjacent to rivers, coasts and in low-lying zones that are more likely to flood. Drivers and pressures include relative wealth, population growth, the provision of food, lifestyle expectations, energy and resource use and climate change. These pose new challenges for the way in which we design our cities of the future.

We live in "yesterday's" cities. Many of the urban patterns that we see today – such as city layouts, buildings, roads and land ownership – are legacies of up to a century and a half of urban policy and decision making, even longer in some of our cities. Tomorrow's cities will also be shaped by the decisions we make today. They must respond to faster changes in physical, social, economic and institutional conditions than previous generations had been used to. Cities are evolving systems. We have little understanding of their behaviour. We know that they are highly dynamic, in that they face changing environments and influences, and adapt to these changes. Over a long period in history, cities have always coped successfully with new environmental conditions and thus have been extremely resilient. From 1100 to 1800, only 42 cities worldwide were deserted at some point after they developed.[1]

Cities everywhere are changing faster than we can assess and understand the diverse forces that cause those changes – these forces themselves are dynamic and fluid. Urban planning on the other hand is relatively static. It is the code by which development decisions are made and therefore by definition an exercise in deciding a city's future form and in so doing giving certainty to the "actors" in that future. Urban planning occurs within a political ideology that informs the decision making process at a given time. Thus to a large extent, we live in "yesterday's cities" in the sense that many of the urban patterns we see today – roads, buildings, land ownership, etc. – reflect decision-making periods of the past. As the prevailing ideology changes so does the planning of our cities. Understanding the role of time and the way it conditions future urban options is a crucial part of urban resilience.

The year 2007 marks a turning point in history: since then, half of the world population has been living in cities.[2] Moreover, the trend of rapid urban growth since the mid-20th century in industrialized countries has now shifted to the developing regions of Asia, Africa and Latin America. Urbanization has led to an increase of economic and social wealth in some places, but also to continuing poverty in others. The urban population is expected to double from 2 to 4 billion over the next 30 to 35 years.[3] These growth rates imply that, every week and over the next four decades, another city will cross the threshold of 1 million inhabitants.

Flooding of the city of Deventer, the Netherlands, in 1995. After the river Meuse floods of 1993 and 1995 the Dutch flood risk management policy has been changed radically. Instead of constraining the rivers between embankments, the new strategy termed "Room for the River" was embraced.

Urban waterfronts, Almere, the Netherlands. Almere is one of the new towns in the Netherlands. In this city water is being appreciated as an indispensable element of the urban environment.

Increasing Flood Vulnerability

Since most of these large cities are located in deltaic regions and other low-lying areas, an unintended side effect of their growth and the ensuing concentration of the number of people there is the increased exposure to floods. Worldwide, the number of dwellers threatened by flooding has increased dramatically. Moreover, floods have become much more frequent and have had more devastating effects than in former times. Indeed, these trends suggest that citizens and urban communities are becoming more vulnerable to floods.

The question arises of how we can dampen this increasing trend of flood vulnerability. Do we know enough about the exposure and sensitivity of cities towards flooding to reveal the underlying processes responsible for this overall increase? Do we understand how cities grow and what the impact of this growth will be on their susceptibility to floods? The answer, unfortunately, is no. In any case, many of the theories of how cities function and grow have been developed in and for industrialized cities, although much of the urban growth of the 21st century is occurring in the developing world. Although comprehensive and systematic research is still lacking a number of studies substantiate the general assumption that urbanization is largely an uncontrolled process. Based on estimates of the United Nations, only 5 percent of new development under way in the world's expanding cities is planned.[4]

Generally speaking, cities are becoming larger and denser. Urban expansion is an issue of serious concern and is often used as a justification for densification. The fundamental question of whether urban expansion should be resisted, accepted

or welcomed is still largely unresolved. From the perspective of flooding, concerns for indiscriminate urban expansion or "sprawl" have captured the attention of both policy makers and academics during the last decade. This is because alongside climate change, it is considered as the major driver for increased flood risk. Sprawl will occur where unplanned, decentralized development dominates as is common in developing countries. Where growth around the periphery of the city is coordinated by strong urban policy, more compact and less vulnerable forms of urban development can be secured. It is evident that these approaches to development have direct consequences for the way floods are managed both in terms of the potential vulnerability of the urban area and its inhabitants, and also in terms of the often indiscriminate effect that urban growth has on run-off and flood probabilities.

At first glance there seem to be conflicting interests between the flood risk managers advocating open, green spaces in their cities and those who are adherents of the compact cities concept as the sustainable urban form that will help to control transport-related greenhouse gas emissions. It follows from the above that there are many theories and concepts on the ideal form of cities and their effectiveness in achieving sustainability; they range from concentration and centralization on the one hand to decentralization with some degree of autonomy on the other. There is, however, no single "magic" recipe for successful planning of a city in response to the challenges of sustainability, climate change and flood risks. Nor is there a single, prescribed sequence of measures, tools, applications and procedures. This is because every city has a unique context.

In many Dutch polders the need for stormwater control, water supply and urban expansion resulted in competing land claims which necessitate the search for multi-functional land-use. Polders such as the Haarlemmermeer and the Zuidplaspolder will accommodate a significant amount of the Randstad's housing growth over the next two decades and about an additional 20 percent of its total surface area is needed for water storage. These renderings of a flood-resilient community at low and high water level show how high density urban developments which are adapted to fluctuating water levels (up to 1 metre) and water storage can be combined in the same area. This has resulted in a structure of compartments containing flood-resilient communities comprised of flood-resilient homes, infrastructure and public green spaces.

Amphibious homes, Maasbommel, the Netherlands, Factor Architects, 2007. The site is located outside the dikes in a recreational area and was chosen for its regularly high water levels. Floods in recent years and subsequent dike reinforcements in the catchment basin have led to the development of houses according to an entirely new concept: houses that only float during floods. To allow the houses to move with the water level, they are built on concrete floating bodies with a coupling construction. At low water level, the houses rest on a concrete foundation. The houses have a wooden frame construction in order to make them as light as possible. To prevent the houses from drifting away during a flood event, they are anchored to flexible mooring posts that cushion the swell of the water. It is expected that once every five years the floodwater will rise to such a level that the houses will lift off the ground. They can accommodate a difference in water level of up to 5.5 metres.

The lack of careful planning, or even uncontrolled building activity, will exacerbate the trend of increasing flood vulnerability of cities due to a combination of the following factors:
1. New "greenfield" development in areas previously in non-urban use, leading to encroachment and expansion onto flood-prone areas, such as flood plains and lowlands;
2. Redevelopment of built-up, previously used areas ("brownfields") and "infill" of the remaining open spaces in them, leading to an overall density increase and subsequent increase of surface sealing and disruption of the natural drainage channels;
3. Urban areas once developed will rarely disappear and tend to favour the status quo, even after major flood disasters. The tabula rasa opportunity for correcting old errors and adopting new approaches to reduce vulnerability is seldom being exploited;
4. Increased dependency on centralised infrastructure systems and utility services; large, centralised systems generally have a greater technical complexity and exhibit greater impact from failure caused by floods than small, decentralised ones. A striking example is the flooding experienced in the United Kingdom in 2007, which caused the loss of piped water for 350,000 people for up to 17 days.

It follows from the above that cities are increasingly losing their capacity to adapt pro-actively to rapid changes, hence their ability to anticipate and deal with floods is diminished. These trends pose new challenges for urban planning and design.

Act of God or Neglect of Man

Historically, natural disasters were viewed as "acts of God", as disruptions to normalcy. Consequently, responses were directed towards managing floods as external events that affected an unsuspecting and unprepared society.[5] Major flood events in the past century, however, have acted as catalysts for changing policies towards floods. They have significantly increased our understanding and capacity to cope with floods.

Although the actual contribution of climate change to losses caused by floods may be marginal compared to the impact of other factors such as the expected growth of urban populations in high-risk areas, in the coming decades climate change will probably have a major influence on the way in which we deal with flooding in the longer term. Countless studies show that we should start now to adapt to climate change, to prevent costly emergency interventions in the future. This means that flood risk management strategies must meet present needs, while providing an adjustment path for the future.[6]

Flood management policies change over time. The transition is a process of predominantly incremental change and reactive responses to flood disasters or flood threats that act as catalysts for accelerating this process. An important notion is that current flood protection measures are based on the accumulated knowledge of past weather events: climate change is perceived as a stationary process (the past serves to predict the future). Major flood disasters have created the need to shift from flood protection to a more integrated approach. In the last decade, however, climate change is recognized as a potential trend breaker, in the way that hydrological variables and existing statistical distributions on flood probabilities are addressed.[7] The present challenge is to recognize that the future is inherently

Floating community "New Arcania", Advin and Dura Vermeer, 1999. This concept for a flood-resilient city was one of the winning entries of a first-of-its-kind Dutch design idea competition aimed at generating innovative solutions for adapting the Netherlands to rising sea levels.

uncertain and that science will not necessarily reduce uncertainty.[8] Climate change with its long-term effect in combination with the current scientific uncertainties[9] poses special challenges. Strategies which address these challenges recognize that there is not one "best solution" but embrace a future which fits into a distribution of events that will not come as a surprise, in other words, where the unexpected is expected. In that sense, climate change provides new incentives to plan ahead and to anticipate extreme events.

Flood Resilience

The concept of resilience is often seen as opposed to the traditional perspectives that attempt to control changes in systems that are perceived as stable. This emerging concept may thus provide guidance for an overarching approach to manage urban floods, which devises strategies to cope with change and uncertainty. Resilience is used quite differently in various fields. Consequently, it has a wide range of connotations. However, there are some unifying features and common notions of resilience. These are:
1. Enhancing resilience is considered a rational strategy to cope with uncertainty and surprise;
2. Resilience is an internal property of (complex, dynamic) systems;
3. Resilient systems have the ability to recover from disturbance (short-term response) and are able to cope with changing conditions (long-term response).[10]

Hence, resilience refers to the capacity to deal with change and continued development (i.e. to adapt and learn). Robustness and flexibility are considered the most relevant mechanisms that enhance resilience. Other (partly overlapping) mechanisms

have also been identified, such as diversity, connectedness, redundancy and information feedbacks. Despite many efforts, we must conclude that currently there is no practical guidance as to how resilience could be made operational for the urban context.

Let us now consider a city from a systems perspective and see how an urban system's resilience (to floods) can be enhanced. An urban system, like many other systems such as living organisms, is structured hierarchically and has emerging properties that cannot be reduced to the properties of the parts ("the whole is greater than the sum of its parts"). As a total approach, the city can be represented as being part of a multi-level interacting system.[11] The city system is made up of various components that take inputs and produce outputs. At a lower spatial level, it is composed of interacting parts or subsystems such as buildings, a transport network and a supporting business environment for organizations to interact. At a higher level, it is part of a supra system, which consists of the entire "catchment area". In principle, at each of these spatial levels, there are three types of measures to reduce the overall system's flood vulnerability based on the type of possible responses of a system to floods. These are reducing exposure, reducing the system's sensitivity and mitigating the impacts (recovery). Flood exposure is directly related to the physical mechanism underlying the flood propagation through the catchment system. The propagation of a flood wave to lower spatial levels is buffered by thresholds that are set at each level. Consequently, flood exposure at a certain spatial level is dependent on the interventions taken at a higher level. In other words, managing flood exposure involves a feedback process that operates top-down. In traditional flood risk management policies, flood exposure

Dordrecht is one of the oldest cities in the Netherlands and is completed surrounded by water. Frequent flooding in the past forced the citizens to adapt their homes to these conditions. Many historical buildings have been made flood proof by using elevated constructions, watertight openings etc.

The Voorstraat, Dordrecht, after the North Sea storm surge of 1953 which devastated vast coastal areas. In the Netherlands, 1,835 people were killed. Delta Works, a flood defence system, arose after this flood.

is generally modified through governmental interventions and restricted to measures taken at the catchment evel only. Reducing the system's sensitivity will reduce either the direct or the indirect impacts, or both. If the urban system is provided with a sufficient amount of redundancy in its attributes, it can switch from one attribute to another. Interventions to reduce sensitivity at a certain level may also enhance the system's redundancy as a whole because of the so-called "ripple effect". Consequently, these interventions will reduce indirect impacts and therefore increase the robustness of the system at a higher spatial level. For example, designing a building that can be made flood-proof could be beneficial for the house owner. A number of such buildings will enhance the city's robustness against floods. Or when a major water utility is knocked out during a flood, other utilities can provide back-up to ensure the delivery of water. In conclusion: urban flood resilience involves multiple spatial levels; resilience approaches are based upon an understanding of the interactions between these levels and they take advantage of the interventions implemented at one level to reduce the system's vulnerability as a whole.

Apart from the spatial dimension of resilience, there is also the dimension of time. Much of the urban fabric and many of the structures we see today are the result of decision-making periods of the past. Shortening lifetime cycles of buildings and infrastructure is one of the means of adapting to long-term changes, correcting old errors and thus increasing flood resilience. In Europe, the building stock is ageing. Within 30 years, approximately one-third of the European building stock will be renewed.[12] Hence, these redevelopment projects may provide a window of opportunity to make adjustments in the urban planning process and to adapt to new conditions.

Urban Design: The Nexus between Theory, Practice and Enabling Institutions

The process that leads to adoption of these innovative views and approaches to cultivate flood resilience on city scale has only just started and research in this field is very limited. Local scale pioneering efforts and experimentation are essential and support the assumption that bottom-up initiatives can shape our cities in a way that they become more flood-resilient. In this multi-faceted and dynamic context, urban design is conceived as the nexus between theory, practice and the enabling institutions. Urban design is the melting pot where ambitions, knowledge and practical experiences come together to deliver flood-resilient developments.

The Dordrecht Urban Flood Management Project is a typical example of such a bottom-up local initiative. The city of Dordrecht, which is one of the oldest cities of the Netherlands, is situated on an island in the Boven Merwede, a part of the river Rhine, and is confronted with the challenge of managing a changing flood risk in its redevelopments and expansions in at-risk areas outside the primary flood defence system. The project revealed that the consequences of flooding in these built-up areas could be minimized through relatively simple individual flood-proofing modifications of traditional buildings and infrastructure. These new, flood-proofing developments could provide an attractive alternative to a physical barrier in the form of an earthen embankment or concrete wall surrounding these developments to further reduce the risk of flooding. Typical features of the urban design entailed "open" waterfronts allowing the citizens to have a splendid panoramic view on the river.

The Dordrecht Urban Flood Management Project. It was found that the consequences of flooding in the flood plains outside the primary flood defence system could be minimized through relatively simple flood-proofing modifications of buildings and infrastructure. Upper plan: planned urban redevelopments; middle plan: Dordrecht during an exceptional flood event, bottom plan: present situation.

Since these built-up areas may provide a safe shelter for the citizens of Dordrecht in case of an exceptional flood (which may result in a flood exposure of a large and dense part of the city area behind the flood defence), the envisaged master plan will also include the design of structures that could be used for vertical evacuation of a large segment of the population.

The Long-term initiatives for flood risk Environments (LifE)[13] approach is an integrated design approach that uses long-term and adaptable non-defence flood risk management responses focussing on a reduction of potential flood impacts instead of solely concentrating on the prevention of flooding. In pratice this means that developments are designed to allow flood water and rainwater into, over or around the sites in a controlled and predetermined manner instead of keeping water out. The intention is to create more adaptable and intuitive landscapes, improving awareness of flood risk and potentially reducing risk to other areas. This innovative approach provides wider benefits to the community; and therefore reduces the economic obstacles to delivering responsible and sustainable developments.[14] The means of managing flood risk explored were designed to have alternative uses for the majority of the time that they were not required to cope with flooding such as attractive green public spaces which act as stormwater storage facilities during periods of extreme precipitation.

The Long-term initiatives for flood risk Environments (LifE) approach is an integrated design approach that uses adaptable non-defence flood risk management responses focussing on a reduction of potential flood impacts instead of solely concentrating on the prevention of flooding. This concept by Baca Architects illustrates options for housing in the various catchment areas.[15]

Upper catchment:
Slow rainwater run-off to reduce pressure on the drains and delay rainwater entering the river. Green roofs and underground storage may be suitable in the floodplain. Ground measures, like swales and rain gardens, may also be used.

Middle catchment:
Let the river flow. Allow the river to flow during a flood by reducing obstacles in the floodplain conveyance. Provide paths for floodwater to return to the river afterwards.

Lower catchment:
Let tides go. Avoid high tides by letting water pass around the site into dedicated flood storage areas. Build in resilience behind defences and emergency escape routes.

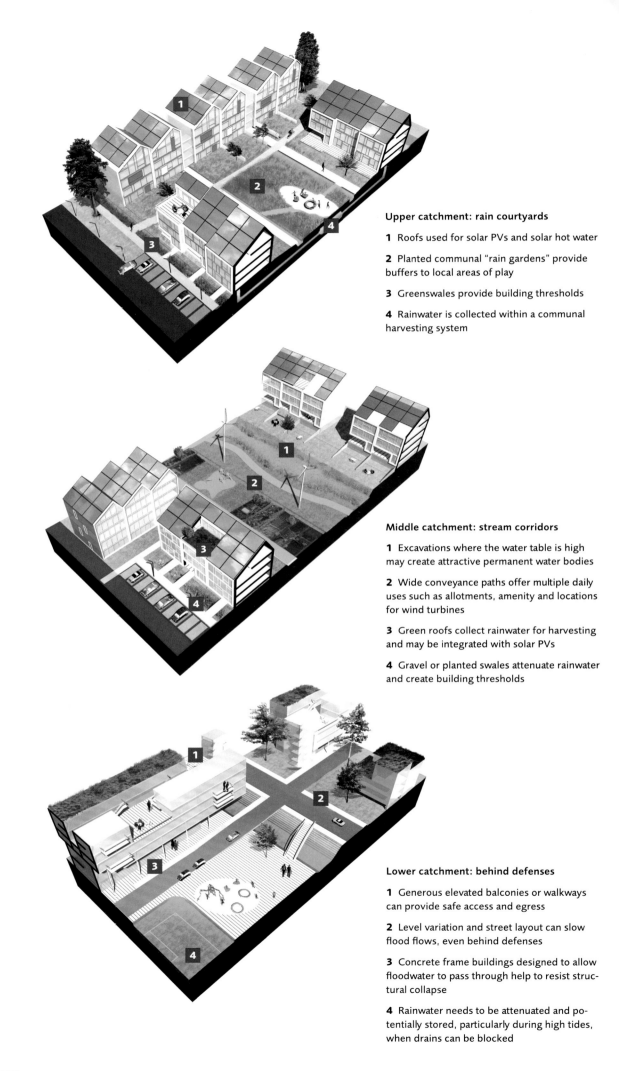

Upper catchment: rain courtyards

1 Roofs used for solar PVs and solar hot water

2 Planted communal "rain gardens" provide buffers to local areas of play

3 Greenswales provide building thresholds

4 Rainwater is collected within a communal harvesting system

Middle catchment: stream corridors

1 Excavations where the water table is high may create attractive permanent water bodies

2 Wide conveyance paths offer multiple daily uses such as allotments, amenity and locations for wind turbines

3 Green roofs collect rainwater for harvesting and may be integrated with solar PVs

4 Gravel or planted swales attenuate rainwater and create building thresholds

Lower catchment: behind defenses

1 Generous elevated balconies or walkways can provide safe access and egress

2 Level variation and street layout can slow flood flows, even behind defenses

3 Concrete frame buildings designed to allow floodwater to pass through help to resist structural collapse

4 Rainwater needs to be attenuated and potentially stored, particularly during high tides, when drains can be blocked

1 B. Allenby and J. Fink, "Viewpoint: Toward inherently secure and resilient societies", *Science*, vol. 309, no. 5737, 2005, pp. 1034-1036.

2 UN-Habitat, "Sustainable Urbanization: Local Actions for Urban Poverty Reduction, Emphasis on Finance and Planning", 21st Session of the Governance Council, 16-20 April, 2007, Nairobi, Kenya.

3 United Nations, "World Population Prospects: The 2005 Revision", United Nation Population Division, Department of Economic and Social Affairs, United Nations, New York, 2006.

4 A. Gentleman, "Architects aren't Ready for an Urbanized Planet", *The International Herald Tribune*, 20 August 2007.

5 J. P. Fleuvrier, "Flood Risk: Education and Folk Memory", *EAT*, special issue "Risques Naturels", 1995, pp. 29–34.

6 Cf. the following publications:
C. Pahl-Wostl (ed.),"Framework for Adaptive Water Management Regimes and for the Transition between Regimes", NeWater project, Report Series, no. 12, 2006.
R. M. Ashley, J. Blanksby, J. Chapman and J. Zhou "Towards Integrated Approaches to Increase Resilience and Robustness for the Prevention and Mitigation of Flood Risk in Urban Areas", in: R. M. Ashley, S. Garvin, E. Pasche, A. Vassilopoulos and C. Zevenbergen (eds.), *Advances in Urban Flood Management*, London: Taylor and Francis, 2007.
R. M. Ashley, "An Adaptable Approach To Flood Risk Management For Local Urban Drainage", Defra Flood and Coastal Erosion Conference, York, 2007.
M. Muller, "Adapting to Climate Change: Water Management for Urban Resilience", *Environment and Urbanization*, no. 19, April 2007, pp. 99-113.

7 Examples of this approach are:
P. Kabat et al., "Climate Proofing The Netherlands", Nature, no. 438, 2005, pp. 283–284.
European Environment Agency – EEA, "Vulnerability and Adaptation to Climate Change in Europe", *Technical Report*, no. 7, 2005, Copenhagen, 2006.

8 See for instance:
R. de Neufville, "Uncertainty Management for Engineering Systems Planning and Design", Engineering Systems Symposium, MIT, 29-31 March 2004.
A. Klinke and O. Renn, "Systematic risks as a challenge for policy making in risk governance", *Forum: Qualitative Social Research*, vol. 7, no. 1, 2006, Art. 33.

9 A distinction is usually made between epistemic and variability uncertainty. The first is due to incomplete knowledge and the second is due to inherent variability. While the epistemic uncertainty can be reduced with measurements, the variability uncertainty represents natural randomness and cannot be reduced.

10 For further information on the concept of resilience, please refer to:
E. Hollnagel, D. D. Woods, N. Leveson, *Resilience Engineering, Concepts and Precepts*, Hampshire: Ashgate Publishing, 2006.
G. C. Gallopin, "Linkages between Vulnerability, Resilience and Adaptive Capacity", *Global Environmental Change*, vol. 16, 2006, pp. 293–303.

11 J. Fiksel, "Sustainability and Resilience: Toward a System Approach", *Sustainability: Science, Practice and Policy*, vol. 2, issue 2, 2006, pp. 14-22

12 ECTP: European Construction Technology Platform, Strategic Research Agenda for the European Construction Sector, 2005.

13 The LifE Project (Long-term Initiatives for Flood-risk Environments) is one of six projects funded by the UK Department for Environment, Food and Rural Affairs (Defra) and its Innovation Fund for Flood and Coastal Erosion Risk Management.

14 Baca Architects and BRE, The LifE Handbook "Long-term initiatives for flood risk environments (LifE)", Defra Innovation project SLD 2318, London: BRE Press, 2009.

15 Upper, middle and lower catchment areas are the three sections along a river, each with certain prevailing hydrological and hydraulic conditions. The upper catchment is often mountainous with small steep streams. Periods of intense rainfall may cause local stormwater flooding. So the emphasis here is on reducing rainwater run-off by retaining the water as much as possible. The middle section is dominated by river flooding; a flood wave coming from upstream may cause flooding of the low-lying floodplains. So here emphasis is on giving the river enough space so that the water can inundate the adjacent land. And the lower part is the area close to the river mouth or delta where the river is wide and slow-flowing. Tides will affect the water level. The strategy here is to tolerate the periodically fluctuating water levels caused or aggravated by the tides.

A Typology of Building on Water
Arts and Culture
Recreation
Living
Industry and Infrastructure

Entrance and central courtyard of Salk Institute for Biological Studies, La Jolla, California, Louis I. Kahn, 1965.

Guggenheim Museum Bilbao, Spain, Frank Gehry, 1997.

Arts and Culture

The waterfront has become a significant location for new building and redevelopment projects, helping cities go beyond their industrial heritage and remaking their image as contemporary places to live and work. Globally, cities are rethinking the treatment of their urban waterfronts as a distinctive element in the social, economic and physical infrastructure of the urban frame. The re-use of obsolete industrial sites is creating new opportunities for cities to reconnect with the water's edge, in addition to providing space for buildings that contribute to recreating a city's identity and international image. For urban theorist Charles Landry, "Whilst amenities like the beauty of a city, health, transport, shopping facilities, cleanliness and parks are important", what stands out above these are the "research capacity, information resources and cultural facilities" that have come to define urban environments.[1]

As American theorist Richard Marshall has noted, "The waterfront is that place in a city where designers and planners can forge contemporary visions of the city and in doing so articulate values that contribute toward urban culture."[2] The high visibility of waterfront projects and their attractiveness can forge new identities for metropolitan areas and allow for an expression of urban vitality that is key to the image of a city. As Marshall asserts, "The waterfront has become the stage or a new expression of city aspirations."[3] Marshall's comments are particularly apt when considering buildings for arts and culture, which offer a platform for exploring creative output from around the world that positions the city at the centre of international debates.

In order to provide a context for this new work, it is useful to note precursors. The Salk Institute for Biological Studies in La Jolla, California is exemplary in this regard. Designed by Louis I. Kahn in 1959–1965, the now infamous educational facility is situated on a coastal bluff overlooking the Pacific Ocean. The building's explicit relationship with its waterfront setting is emphasized not only through its location but also in the orientation of the building and its public spaces that provide sightlines out to the water. The image that is most associated with this structure is the majestically proportioned exterior courtyard, sliced in two by a narrow channel of water. When viewed from certain angles, the water appears to run off the edge of the site and into the ocean below. However, on reaching the edge of the site it becomes clear that the water runs down the edge of the plaza and cascades into a series of pools below; a metaphor for the infinite expanse of the Pacific Ocean. Water gives the building a poetic expression and it is the element that frames and defines this architectural setting and creates a place of contemplation and activity in keeping with the mission of this research facility.

The architect perhaps most recognized for creating buildings that intersect with water, however, is the Japanese designer Tadao Ando. Seminal projects such as the Water Temple built in 1989–1991 in Hompukuji, Japan, a small town in the northern part of Awaji Island, illustrate Ando's ability to bring people into a spatial relationship with water. Sitting amidst a hilly landscape, the temple is buried beneath an elliptical pool of water. The pool is protected from views to the front by a curved concrete wall that channels visitors to the entrance that descends into the centre of the lily pond. On the rear side, the pool extends out to the natural environment and overlooks the rice paddies, mountains and sea. The sanctuary below ground mirrors the shape of the pond above. An ovoid pool sunk in the earth also marks Ando's design of the Naoshima Contemporary

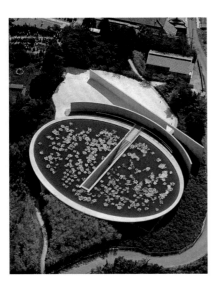

Aerial view of The Water Temple,
Awaji Island, Japan, Tadao Ando,
1991.

Aerial view of Chichu Art Museum, Naoshima, Kagawa, Japan,
Tadao Ando, 2004.

Art Museum opened in 1995 in Naoshima, Japan. Ando inverts the relationship between the land and the body of water that surrounds it by bringing water onto the island. The island of Naoshima is also the location of another Ando building, the Chichu Art Museum. Ando's designs are potent sensory experiences that build on an historical trajectory in Japan of the physical and spiritual benefits of water and its relationship to architecture.

More conspicuous in its relationship to water both physically and metaphorically, is the Guggenheim in Bilbao, Spain by Frank Gehry. Deemed by architect Philip Johnson as "the greatest building of our time" when it opened in 1997, the museum remains a cornerstone of discussions focused on the revitalization of cities through iconic architecture.[4] Built on the site of a former shipyard along the river Nervión, the building was engineered as the linchpin of renewal efforts in Bilbao following its economic decline in the 1960s and 1970s when the city's manufacturing industry collapsed and Bilbao suffered from high unemployment and environmental decay. In 1980, five years after the death of Spain's military dictator Francisco Franco, the Basque Country became a semi-autonomous region. Energized by the possibility of determining a new future for itself, the city began to reposition its economy, moving away from its industrial foundation towards establishing itself as a centre of financial services and telecommunications. The Guggenheim was envisioned as a beacon for the city's transformation. Reminiscent of a docked cruise ship and surfaced in a reflective metal skin, the building connects the design to the city's role as a former industrial port. However, the sweeping sculptural form of the building and the use of titanium as a building material point to a new future for the city envisioned through contemporary art and design with tourism in its wake.

Despite attempts to emulate the "Bilbao effect" elsewhere in the world, very few new museums or galleries outside capital cities have succeeded in getting so many visitors. In its first year, 100,000 people visited the museum a month. Since then, the museum has clocked approximately 1 million visitors per year proving Marshall McLuhan's adage that "the medium is the message". In the same year the National Centre for Science and Technology (NEMO), designed by Italian architect Renzo Piano, opened to critical acclaim in Amsterdam. The building bears an explicit relationship to its waterfront setting in the harbour area of the northern section of Amsterdam. Clad in copper, the boat-shaped structure stands out against the skyline. Its sloping roof is a direct response to the site and provides a roof terrace and viewing platform for visitors overlooking the harbour and city. Equally prominent in relation to the urban frame is the expansion of the 100-year-old Groninger Museum in Groningen in the Netherlands, opened three years earlier, in 1994. The complex of different structures that house the museum's sprawling collection of antiquities to Modern Art was conceived by Italian architect Alessandro Mendini who also designed the centrepiece building. Additional wings were designed by Philippe Starck, Michele De Lucchi, and Coop Himmelb[l]au. The unusual grouping of colourful angular postmodernist structures signal the diversity of the museum's holdings. Fronted by the Verbindings Canal, the buildings respond to the disconnected site by forming a bridge between the main railway station and the inner city.

In other cities, the adaptive re-use of formerly industrial buildings on waterfront settings is providing opportunities for new activities at the water's edge. In London, large areas of the city along the South Bank, the brownfields of the Greenwich

Groninger Museum, Groningen, the Netherlands, 1994.
The museum consists of three volumes: a silver cylindrical building
designed by Philippe Starck, a yellow tower by Alessandro Mendini,
and a pale blue pavilion by Coop Himmelb(l)au.

National Centre for Science and Technology NEMO, Amsterdam,
the Netherlands, Renzo Piano Building Workshop, 1997.

Peninsula, and the Docklands have been steadily undergoing
renewal. Perhaps the most pivotal regeneration project to date
is the recasting of the former Bankside Power Station into the
Tate Modern in 2000, made especially popular by the design
and construction of the Millennium Bridge. Despite its rocky
start (the bridge was closed soon after opening, modified,
and later reopened when crowds experienced an unexpected
swaying motion), the overpass has serviced thousands of visitors who can cross the river Thames on foot entering near St.
Paul's Cathedral and exiting near the museum. The bridge also
creates one of the best places from which to view the city and
the new waterfront developments, mid-river.

The design of Tate Modern, by Swiss architects Herzog & de
Meuron, retains the colossal shell of the industrial facility but
upgrades it to a museum of modern art, capping it with a glass
box that glows from within at night, attracting visitors to this
formerly abandoned riverside location during the day and into
the evening. So successful has the new museum been (2006
was a record-breaking year for the museum when 5 million visitors attended exhibitions and programmes, making it London's
most popular tourist attraction) that it is currently engaged in
expansion plans. A pyramidal structure of stacked boxes, also
the vision of Herzog & de Meuron, is planned for a site adjacent to the original building and expected to open in 2012.
This multi-level addition will house further exhibition, educational and office spaces. Other cultural buildings, landscaping
and public spaces are also envisioned as part of a larger master
plan, which will result in a new cultural quarter to the south
of the river Thames anchored by Tate Modern.

In 2003, the revered Royal Library of Alexandria in Egypt in-
augurated its new building designed by Oslo-based architects
Snøhetta. The firm's first major commission, the vast compound
contains a reading room laid out across eleven levels as well as
a conference centre, museums, art galleries, a planetarium and
a manuscript restoration laboratory. Most striking about the
design is its relationship to its waterfront setting. The building
emerges from a reflecting pool of water. Its sloping roof, which
stands at 32 metres high, is angled to the adjacent coastline
and has been likened to a giant sundial.

Other cities have anchored urban renewal efforts to major cultural events. The 1992 Olympics in Barcelona were an essential
springboard for redeveloping the Port Vell (Old Port), at the
base of the Rambla. In 2004, another large event, the Universal
Forum of Cultures, a UNESCO congress, was utilized to spear-
head the transformation of the Poblenou area to the east of the
city and generated new architecture such as exhibition space
and conference centres on the seafront by a host of international architects including Herzog & de Meuron, MVRDV and
Jean Nouvel.

In 2006, the America's Cup helped retool the Playa de Levante
Beachfront in Valencia, Spain. A pavilion designed by UK architect David Chipperfield became the focal point of this annual
yachting event. Conceptualized and built in eleven months,
the streamlined forms takes advantage of its waterfront setting,
engaging the landscape through a series of cantilevered decks
that provide unobstructed views across the water and reach
out at a single point to touch the beach below.

The Blur Building media pavilion by Diller Scofidio + Renfro for Swiss Expo 2002 on Lake Neuchâtel in Yverdon-les-Bains, Switzerland.

The Blur Building was inspired by Buckminster Fuller structures and consisted of a tensegrity system of rectilinear struts and diagonal rods cantilevered out over the lake, accessed by ramps. Filtered lake water shot as a fine mist through 13,000 fog nozzles and created an artificial cloud that responded to changing weather conditions.

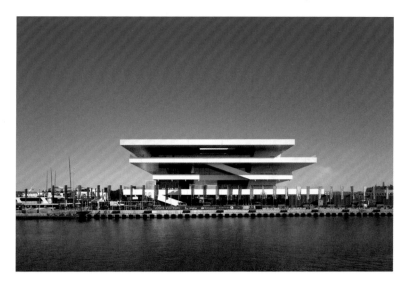

America's Cup Building, Valencia, Spain, David Chipperfield, 2006.

British Pavilion, Expo '92, Seville, Spain, Nicholas Grimshaw, 1992.

In addition to designing on waterfront sites, water as an essential component of the design of buildings for environmental, technological, social and aesthetic reasons has been the focus of inventive architectural designs and has opened up new areas for debate within the fields of architecture and design.

In 1992, for example, the main attraction of the British Pavilion at Expo '92 in Seville, Spain was a 65-metre-long and 18-metre-high water wall, which illustrated the potential of passive cooling technology as a method of controlling the climatic conditions within the public spaces of the pavilion. Designed by architect Nicholas Grimshaw in collaboration with William Pye Partnership, water was pumped up to the top of the structure from where it cascaded down the exterior east wall to great visual effect, reducing the surface temperature of the building and therefore helping to cool the interior.

Using water as a material element was also at the heart of the Hydra Pier, a multi-media pavilion designed by New York-based Asymptote for the Floriade in Haarlemmermeer, the Netherlands, in 2002. The building is sited on an artificial lake. During the Dutch horticultural fair that takes place every ten years, a thin film of water was pumped over the aluminum roof, free-falling over the edges and down the sides of the building. The curtain wall of water was both a symbolic gesture about the boundaries of land and water and an element that provided a cooling mechanism. The constant flow of water added a sensuous element to the design and meant the façade was continuously animated in a play of light and movement.

The potential for water to dematerialize the architectural structure of a building was the driving force behind Diller Scofidio + Renfro's Blur Building installed in 2002 as part of the Swiss Expo. Water literally became the material construct of the building's surface. The pavilion, which visitors could enter, was made from a lightweight steel tensegrity structure, measuring approximately 90 metres wide by 60 metres deep by 23 metres high, on Lake Neuchâtel in Yverdon-les-Bains. Water, pumped from the lake, was filtered and shot as a fine mist through 31,500 high-pressure mist nozzles. A smart weather system read the shifting conditions of temperature, humidity, wind speed and direction, and processed the data in a central computer that regulated water pressure. The design team summed up their project as an "architecture of atmosphere".

Other projects have investigated the potential of new media as a component part of the architecture, defining experiential elements in space which apply digital and simulation technologies to rushing water. The Digital Water Pavilion, a project commissioned for the 2008 EXPO in Zaragoza, Spain, and developed in concert with MIT's SENSEable City Laboratory and the Media Lab's Smart Cities research group by William J. Mitchell, infused a curtain wall made of water with morphing geometries determined by computer-fed data. These liquid and shape-shifting membranes created a dynamic entrance to the fair. Elsewhere at the EXPO, 5,000 litres of water per minute were circulated through the Tower of Water (Torre del Agua) pavilion to create interactive displays choreographed by Program Collective with designers in Barcelona, London and Chicago. In the tower, rushing water merged with digital projections revealing macro-to-microscopic patterns and scales of water, further intensifying the atmospheric quality of the pavilion. Both projects alluded to the importance of water in our lives and its role as a dynamic element in architecture and the design of cities.

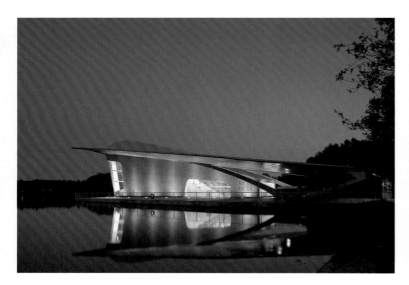

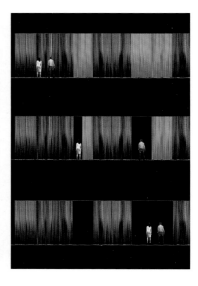

Hydra Pier, Haarlemmermeer, the Netherlands, Asymptote, 2002. The pavilion was commissioned for the Floriade exhibition, a once-a-decade Dutch horticultural fair. The pumping of water through and onto the roof and the 3.5-metre-high curtain of water that acted as an entry threshold celebrates the surrounding landscape that was below sea level for most of the 19th century.

A visitor to the Tower of Water (Torre del Agua) pavilion at EXPO 2008 designed by Program Collective in Zaragoza, Spain, interacts with the "water-curtain", a mutable surface of real water that is digitally enhanced.

A conceptual storyboard for the "water-curtain", that combines rushing water, digital projections and computer-programmed interactive openings that together define an experiential threshold within the Tower of Water.

The arts and culture buildings in this book are all sited in areas rapidly undergoing an urban renaissance. They illustrate a diversity of experience through the design of the architecture, which is responsive to the context of the urban frame and the relationship to the built environment and the water. The Hamburg Science Centre forms part of a harbour-wide regeneration project aimed at stimulating this formerly industrial neighbourhood. In the case of the Institute of Contemporary Art in Boston, the new museum is a physical manifestation of the attempt to visually and physically connect the city's bustling downtown area and its waterfront, prompting area-wide redevelopment. Likewise, the Oslo National Opera House functions as both an arresting new cultural centre and meeting point for this steadily evolving corner of the city.

As urban theorist Jane Jacobs has acknowledged in what are now a well-known suite of volumes about urban planning and design, the city is only as interesting as its streets and public spaces. I would add the same for its architecture. What Jacobs and fellow urban critics including Richard Marshall and Charles Landry emphasize is the importance of a diversity of spaces and places with multidimensional character that will encourage the interplay of people and ideas. As Landry maintains, new cultural facilities and activities are "significant factors in generating inspiration, self-confidence, debate or ideas exchange as well as the creation of a city's image."[5]

Recreation

Recreational spaces are essential to the health of cities and rural areas, providing places for cross-generational relaxation and exchange. As critic Tracy Metz has noted, "Leisure is more than the time that you can spend as you like ... Our social identity is determined by the way we spend our leisure at least as much as by the work we do or the possessions we own ... We want to be stimulated, we want to enjoy, to experience something, to try out everything ..."[6] New recreational venues on waterfronts are radically altering the landscape of cities and providing opportunities for engaging with water. From sitting on a river bank and letting the water run through one's fingers to more active endeavours such as swimming and boating to dining en plein air, people increasingly seek out opportunities to be close to water.

Throughout history, recreational venues such as the water gardens at the Villa d'Este in Tivoli, near Rome, completed in 1560, and the popular amusement park Tivoli Gardens, opened in Copenhagen, have attracted visitors due to their water-based activities. More recent examples such as Emscher Park in the Ruhr valley of northwestern Germany, opened in 1999, and Westergasfabriek Park in Amsterdam, 2003, have transformed formerly industrial waterways into major recreational and cultural destinations with activities that take advantage of the natural landscape. Other recreational venues integrate water as a component part of the design.

In addition to parks and plazas, architectural projects sited on the water offer a diversity of recreational spaces that can accommodate a range of people and activities in an effort to foster play, relaxation, education and interaction: all essential aspects of daily life.

The Spree Bridge Bathing Ship (covered by a roof in winter, Wilk-Salinas Architek-ten, 2005), re-cycles an old river barge into an urban swimming pool along the banks of the river Spree in Berlin, Germany.

The Avenue of the One Hundred Fountains (Le Cento Fontane) at the Villa d'Este, Tivoli near Rome, Italy, 1560.

Tivoli Gardens in Denmark, opened in the summer of 1843, is one of the oldest amusement park in the world.

Floating Swimming Pool, Brooklyn, New York, Jonathan Kirschenfeld Associates, 2007.

Paris Plage transforms the capital city in the summer into a car-free zone with places for relaxation and sports activities along the banks of the river Seine.

The Spree Bridge Bathing Ship in Berlin provides an opportunity to be on the river Spree, and the outdoor swimming pool and sunbathing deck reinvents the public life of the riverfront, shifting it away from heavy industry towards recreational uses. Made from an old cargo container, the swimming pool is anchored in the eastern area of the harbour. The 32-metre-long barge is filled with freshwater that gives the impression of swimming in the river. The project was conceived of by curator Heike Catherina Müller of the public art organization Stadtkunstprojekte e.V. In 2002, Müller organized a design competition for ideas linking the city to the river Spree through public art projects in and around existing bridges. AMP Arquitectos from Tenerife and Berlin-based architects Gil Wilk and artist Susanne Lorenz won the competition with their innovative idea to create a new bridge for the river in the shape of an urban marine bath. Opened in 2004, the project has proved to be a popular site for residents and visitors alike. In 2005, a roof was added (Wilk-Salinas Architekten), which is made from an air-filled plastic tube that encloses the pool and deck areas, making the pool habitable as a sauna and lounge during the winter months.

A similar project in New York builds on the city's history of river bathhouses that were stationed along the edge of Manhattan from the 1870s to the 1940s. In 2007, a floating swimming pool was once again docked in Brooklyn for the summer. The idea, more than 20 years in the making, was the brainchild of Ann L. Buttenwieser, a former parks department official, who has been working to finance the pool through the Neptune Foundation, a nonprofit group she founded for the project. Jonathan Kirschenfeld Associates' design recalls earlier bathhouses from the 19th century in its linear layout complete with locker rooms, showers, a snack bar, and areas for small gatherings.

Artificial beachscapes have also become something of a calling card for cities during the summer months. One of the most successful projects is the Paris Plage that launched in 2002 in France's capital city and that each year has transformed the area around the Right Bank into a beach during the hottest weeks of the year. The idea, spearheaded by Mayor Bertrand Delanoë, was specifically geared towards residents who are not able, because of time and resource restraints, to leave the city during the summer. Scenographer Jean-Christophe Choblet was hired to create the "stage" for the beach, which covers a 3-kilometre section of the Georges Pompidou expressway. Beach umbrellas, "parabrume" fog machines, lounge chairs, palm tress and tonnes of sand shipped in every summer create areas for sunbathing and for sports such as beach volleyball, as well as areas for concerts and film projections. The beach is a major success story for the city and has inspired others to follow suit, including Amsterdam, Berlin, Brussels, Budapest and Rome.

Since 1999, the Young Architects Forum organized by the Museum of Modern Art and PS1 contemporary art centre in New York has provided a forum for emerging architects to design an experimental landscape for relaxation and performances. Although not installed by a natural body of water but in the courtyard of PS1 in Long Island City, the project has become a destination for city dwellers for its innovative design which includes water elements that encourage visitor interaction. In 2000, for instance, SHoP Architects from New York created an undulating wooden decked surface with seating areas and shallow pools for lounging and paddling.

Dunescape, a summer courtyard installation designed by
SHoP Architects for PS1/MoMA's Young Architects' Program,
Long Island City, New York, 2000.

The Red Sea Star Underwater Restaurant, Bar and Observatory
off the coast of Eilat, Israel, Ayala Serfaty, 1999.

Many of these projects were initiated as getaway destinations in the city for residents during the summer months. They illustrate the inherent possibilities for new and unexpected experiences that are an intrinsic part of our urban environments. As the authors of Urban Pioneers, a book exploring interventions in public space attest, such projects have the potential to contribute to the "social and economic foundations of urban society" as well as promote regeneration and a "lively cityscape". Although often logistically complex and at times costly, the results can be overwhelmingly positive, providing new landscapes that engage the community and promote social cohesion. In addition, they can help alleviate the negative effects of post-industrial decay and introduce a renewed image of a city by triggering positive developments that can have an impact on an entire district.

The recreation facilities explored in this book are often successful generators of urban and suburban renewal. These projects provide new meeting and gathering spaces, activity zones and areas of relaxation that bring people together to share experiences that are an antidote to our increasingly structured and complex daily lives.

The Island in the Mur, a performance and playground space designed by Acconci Studio based in New York, was commissioned for the year-long celebration of art and culture in Graz, Austria, in 2003. The shell-like form reinterprets traditional floating performance venues on barges and provides a bridge across the river as well as an area for theatre performances and a children's playground.

For centuries, the design of spas has exploited relationships between architecture and water. In Roman times, bathing was an essential aspect of daily life. Classically designed public baths provided places for communal bathing and socializing. Their design is discussed in Vitruvius' volume De Architectura thought to be written in 15 BC. In the Middle East, the Turkish bath or hamam, a variant of a steam bath, has also played an important role in society. Made popular during the reign of the Ottoman Empire, the hamam became a central location for meeting and gathering in cities as well as a place for cleansing. Today, spa resorts offer opportunities to take advantage of the recuperative and life-enhancing benefits of spring water. What distinguishes Nicholas Grimshaw's design for the Thermae Spa from other contemporary spas built in recent years, including the well-known Therme Vals, completed in 1996, and designed by the Swiss architect Peter Zumthor, is its response to a specific historic setting. Unlike the rural location of Therme Vals in the Swiss Alps, the Thermae Spa is located in Bath, a town in Southern England that is located on the site of a former spa where people have benefited from England's only natural thermal waters for 2,000 years.

Eateries on waterfront settings never fail to delight in their proximity to water. Spectacular examples include the celebrated Red Sea Star Restaurant off the coast of Eilat in Israel, design by Tel Aviv-based designer Ayala Serfaty, and located 5 metres below sea level with windows that look out to the adjacent sea life. Although more humble in scale, the East Beach Café featured in this book stands out as an innovative new take on the traditional white-washed wooden huts that serve simple fare to holidaymakers along the sea coasts of England.

Therme Vals, Switzerland, Peter Zumthor, 1996.

Thermae Spa, Bath, Great Britain, Nicholas Grimshaw, 2006.

National Assembly Complex Sher-e-Bangla Nagar, Dhaka, Bangladesh, Louis I. Kahn, 1962–1983.

Capitol Complex, Chandigarh, India, Le Corbusier, 1964.

Living

According to Dutch artist Hans Venhuizen, "Amphibious living is housing that is optimally adjusted" to different bodies of water "by responding as much as possible to the special qualities of these conditions."[7] Although his comments refer to temporary or mobile floating dwellings they could equally relate to more permanent homes located on water for use year-round. As Paul Meurs asserts, "The arrival of economic growth and the development of technology provided building with virtually unlimited possibilities. In the 20th century it suddenly became possible to build anywhere."[8]

Throughout history our living spaces have been built with a symbiotic relationship to their setting whether for environmental, aesthetic, and social reasons, or for protection. In Europe, for centuries castles have been built on rivers or lined by man-made moats filled with water, which kept out all but the most determined intruders. Leeds Castle, for example, designed by Robert de Crevecoeur was built for King Edward I in 1119 on two islands in the river Len in southeast England. The stone castle replaced an earlier wooden structure on the site. The original wooden drawbridges were substituted by stone causeways, defended by a series of towers that were added to the design of the castle. Further along the southern coast of England in East Sussex, Bodiam Castle, a medieval quadrangular castle built in East Sussex in 1385 by Sir Edward Dalyngrigge, a former knight of Edward III, is also surrounded by a moat. Château Chenonceau in the Loire Valley in France, completed in 1521 on the site of an old mill and castle, is a more unusual example. Commissioned by Thomas Bohier, Chamberlain for King Charles VIII of France, the building, rather than centred

on water, spans the river Cher like a bridge with arches at its lowest level. A gallery runs from one end of the building to the other at its centre. However, like its predecessors, the castle is defined by the river that surrounds it on all sides. Now accessed by stone bridges, the castle was originally accessed by wooden drawbridges on either side of the river. Castles and forts in the Eastern hemisphere are also characterized by elaborate moats. The Japanese Imperial Palace in Tokyo, for example, completed in 1888 but destroyed during World War II and rebuilt afterwards in the same style, is surrounded by a moat which is used extensively today, catering to leisure boats, fishing and restaurants. The Forbidden City, the Chinese imperial palace from the mid-Ming Dynasty to the end of the Qing Dynasty, is also surrounded by a moat. Built from 1406 to 1420, the complex has been under the charge of the Palace Museum since 1924, and its grounds, including the 6-metre-deep and 52-metre-wide body of water, now make up a public park.

The relationship between architecture and water has a potent history in Asia. Major influences stem from Zen Buddhism, which calls for the built and natural environments to come together in a seamless fusion of interior and exterior spaces as a metaphor for the mind. As James Wines writes, the Zen Mandara (a theological coda), "proposes a doctrine of dual realms—one being 'the principle and the cause', the other being 'the intelligence and the effect'." In other words, as Wines explains, "The Mandara was the symbolic reference to a psychic state in which the mind became a landscape, achieving a fusion with nature and a perfect peace and spirituality."[9] In early examples of Asian architecture, interior and exterior spaces are fused

Leeds Castle, near Kent, England, is surrounded by a moat. The castle dates back to 1119 and was originally built by Robert de Crevecoeur to replace an earlier Saxon manor.

Bodiam Castle in East Sussex, southern England, built in 1385, is an example of a late medieval moated castle.

The 11th-century Château de Chenonceau near the small village of Chenonceaux in the Loire Valley, France, was built on the site of an old mill on the river Cher.

The Imperial Palace in Tokyo, Japan, originally built in 1888, is a park-like area with multiple buildings, surrounded by pools of water, and is the main residence of the Emperor of Japan.

A decorative pool at the Katsura Imperial Villa, Kyoto, Japan, 1650.

The Taj Mahal in Agra, India, built around 1653.

into one another through the use of open-plan spatial organizations and by borrowing elements from the outdoors for use indoors, such as stone and wood and other natural materials, as well as the inclusion of water features and small reflecting pools. The numerous buildings that make up the Royal Palace of Katsura in Kyoto, Japan (completed in 1650) are carefully constructed around a pond created from the water of the river Katsura-gawa. The idea was to create a microcosmic form of life within one setting. The delineation of outdoor living rooms that reflected those created indoors also played a fundamental role in Zen Buddhist architecture. Wooden screens and other architectural elements were used to partition off areas for contemplation and relaxation complete with outdoor seating arrangements. According to Wines, "Zen was not about gardening, or relating to nature from a purely observational perspective, but rather it was about the act of being nature", through the symbiosis of architecture and nature.[10]

In India, a strong relationship between architecture and water has existed for centuries, whether for defense purposes, in the case of palaces, or as recreational venues in the case of pools and adjacencies to rivers and streams. These bodies of water also provide natural ventilation from cool breezes that sweep across the surface. Decorative pools in front of palaces such as the Taj Mahal in Agra were also favoured for their reflective properties, making buildings appear grander in scale. During events such as religious festivals they were bedecked with candles and lamps marking these special occasions. "Whilst in the religious context the metaphysical purity and the sacredness of water played an important role, in a palace context the physical purity of the water and the joy of looking at water... seem to have been of higher importance."[11]

In the 20th century, water architecture continued to sustain an important place in Asia. Le Corbusier, for example, incorporated large bodies of water into the design of the Capital Complex in Chandigarh, completed in 1964. Hegewald asserts that "From certain view-points, these basins convey the illusion that the Palace of Assembly and the High Court are floating on water."[12] She also points to Louis Kahn's design for the Capital Complex Shere-Bangla Nagar in Dhaka, Bangladesh built 1962–1983 as a later example planned within and around a water reservoir.

Other architects such as Frank Lloyd Wright rose to prominence for designs rooted in techniques drawn from Asian architecture (that he is known to have visited and studied) but applied to a Western context. His designs are derived from an organic architecture that was in harmony with nature. In 1936, for example, he gained recognition for Fallingwater, a house built in a rural setting in Bear Run, Pennsylvania for Edgar J. Kaufmann, a successful Pittsburgh businessman and founder of Kaufmann's Department Store. The former weekend residence, now the property of the Western Pennsylvania Conservancy and open to the public, is an example of Wright's interest in creating an organic architecture that is in harmony with nature. The design of Falling Water, as its name suggests, called for the house to be built over a waterfall. Cantilevered terraces that resemble nearby rock formations extend into the heavily wooded area, mirroring the planes of the land and creating connections between the immediate surroundings and the house. The house has an inherent connection to its location both physically and visually through the topography of the structure and the use of materials, often indigenous to the site. The construction of the house also heightens these relationships. The glass and stone

Lovell Beach House, Newport Beach, California, USA,
Rudolf Schindler, 1926.

Fallingwater, Bear Run, Pennsylvania, USA, Frank Lloyd Wright, 1936.

walls that rise from the floor to the ceiling meet head-on rather than first framed in metal. They therefore create an illusion of a seamless flow between the interior and exterior spaces.

On the West Coast of America, the Lovell Beach House, completed in 1926, also stands as an example of a residential building that directly relates to its waterfront setting. Built in Newport Beach, California, the horizontal lines and cantilevered planes of the structure are reminiscent of the architecture of Frank Lloyd Wright for whom the designer Rudolph Schindler had worked earlier in the century. The clear organization of the western elevation of the house facing the ocean provides open living quarters with panoramic views over the water. Elevating the building above the ground on stilts allows the beach to permeate the area underneath the house and provides a sheltered space for outdoor activities.

Although architects around the world have continued to interrogate and challenge the interrelationship between architecture and water through new living dwellings, the Netherlands is one of the most forward-thinking countries in terms of building on water. The Dutch have fought against flooding for centuries, developing dikes and sophisticated pumping systems to keep water at bay. Based on necessity as well as ecological imperatives, with one-third of the country resting below sea level, architects across Holland continue to rethink traditional strategies for new housing communities built on water-locked landscapes.

In the last decade of the 20th century the Eastern Docklands, a former harbour district in Amsterdam, for example, was earmarked as the site for new residential development. In 2000, Dutch urban designers and landscape architects West 8 designed the allocation of 2,500 dwellings on the Borneo and Sporenburg peninsulas to the north of the city that generated a mixture of building typologies from densely packed apartment buildings to houses with patios. Currently in development is a new residential district, IJburg, located on seven artificial islands built on the IJmeer lake on Amsterdam's eastern side. The islands were built on land made from dredged sand, sprayed layer after layer into the open water of the IJmeer freshwater lake. When complete, the islands will be home to some 45,000 city-dwellers in 18,000 dwellings. The project, initially started in 1996, was put on hold a year later after growing concerns about the ecological implications of the project. Following intensive research, but inconclusive evidence, a referendum followed in 1997 and the project was reinstated based on an urban plan completed in 1996 by the firm of Palmboom & Van den Bout. The first buildings were completed in 2002 on the Haveneiland, and the IJ tram began servicing the area in 2005.

In Almere, a city in the centre of the Netherlands, a series of experimental housing communities built on the Ijsselmeer polders, low-lying tracts of land enclosed by dikes are providing a case study for the creation of a new dense community of flexible dwellings. The 48 water villas built in 2001 and designed by UN Studio are mindful of their locale. The first floor of each unit juts out to create a glass-fronted balcony, which directs natural light into the loft-like spaces and provides unobstructed views across the landscape.

Aerial views of Borneo Sporenburg, a residential district master-planned by West 8 on the Eastern Docklands in Amsterdam, the Netherlands. The first buildings were completed in 2002.

Detail view of a circular housing block on Borneo Sporenburg.

Water Villas, Almere, the Netherlands, UN Studio, 2001.

Proposal for an outdoor museum for the Ark of the World Foundation in Carara National Park, Costa Rica, Greg Lynn, concept 2002.

Student proposal for a water residence on legs designed by Edmund Carter, Nikita Shah and Ashvin Bhargava, 2005.

In Costa Rica, the dense environment of the rainforest offers an engaging setting for innovative building projects. Los Angeles-based Greg Lynn's Ark of the World is an interesting case study. The vividly-hued structure that sits over an artificial lake on the border of the Carara National Park derives its form from native tropical plant and flower life. The bulbous shape of the museum is realized through computer modeling software of the sort for which Lynn has become famed. The Ark of the World, a project still in the conceptual phase, houses a natural history museum, ecology visitor's centre and contemporary art museum. The organic form of the building nestles into the environment like an exotic flower. Its lurid green tendrils extend across the water, creating connections with the land.

Living by the water has its perks: panoramic views, natural landscape settings and opportunities for water-based activities. However, it also poses a host of challenges, including the potential for flooding. In May 2005, Greg Lynn also taught a master class focused on flood-resistant housing with 60 architecture students from the Rotterdam Academy of Architecture and Urban Design, the Delft University of Technology, the International Architecture Biennale Rotterdam, the Netherlands Architecture Institute and the Berlage Institute. The workshop focused on Deventer in the Netherlands, an area at risk of flooding, as a case study for investigations.

Stacey Thomas, Tina Jelenc, Chintan Raveshia, and Florian Heinzelmann conceived Asteroid, a sculptural building with a faceted surface of glass panels that rises and falls with floodwaters, providing views over the land in dry seasons and over the water in wet seasons. Edmund Carter, Nikita Shah and Ashvin Bhargava's design is no less eye-catching. The crustacean-like shell of the dwelling is a lightweight structure that floats above the water on a tripod arrangement of elongated legs that enables the building to rise and fall with tidal changes. These futuristic designs are reminiscent of the visionary structures of designers such as Ron Herron, a member of Archigram who proposed "Walking City" in 1964, a giant, self-contained living pod that could roam the landscape. Likewise, the Waterbug, as its name suggests takes inspiration from the natural world to provide alternative solutions to new housing that are adaptive to change caused by fluctuating environmental conditions.

As architects are creating ever more advanced systems for contemporary living, US architect and artist James Wines asserts that "the aesthetic value of buildings should no longer be seen exclusively as a sculptural art of abstract form, space, and structure, but should, rather, shift the focus to informational and contextual associations relating more to a dialogue in the mind." Wines calls on architects to consistently work to redefine the discipline by opening it up to fresh ideas and approaches that are responsive and in tune to changes in contemporary life. He concludes that buildings should be "seen as a means of critical commentary on the basic definition of architecture, buildings as hybrid fusions of representation and abstraction, and buildings as 'environmental sponges', which absorb their imagistic clues from the widest possible range of contextual sources."[13]

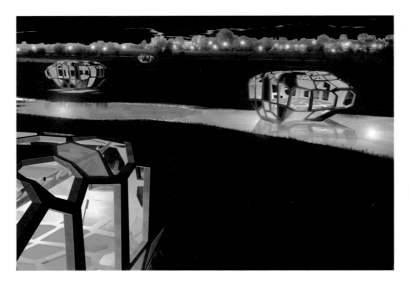

Student proposal Asteroid, a new type of flood-resistant house designed by Stacey Thomas, Tina Jelenc, Chintan Raveshia and Florian Heinzelmann, 2005.

Yokohama International Port Terminal, Yokohama, Japan, Foreign Office Architects, 2002.

Wines' comments are echoed in the groundbreaking projects explored in this book that provide examples of the diversity of dwellings built on and by water. Sited on the San Francisco Bay, for instance, the Jellyfish House by IwamotoScott Architecture makes use of smart technologies to tackle brownfield site remediation, re-cycles and purifies greywater run-off, and generates its own passive heating and cooling mechanisms in an effort to create a self-sustaining organism for habitation.

French designers Erwan and Ronan Bouroullec's Maison Flottante, a floating structure that draws inspiration from houseboats and log cabins, doubles as a studio and living unit for artists-in-residents at Cneai, a contemporary art institution in Paris.

On Lake Huron in Ontario, Canada, MOS Architects considered the logistics of the volatile site in their design for an elegant wooden summerhouse that floats on the water, rising and falling with the tide.

On a larger scale is Mass Studies' Seoul Commune. Like the Silodam residential housing block designed by MVRDV and also discussed, Seoul Commune aims to introduce a new type of interactive, communal-style living in which public spaces are shared throughout the building, offering opportunities for interaction and exchange. The striking cluster of high-rise structures has been conceived as a model of sustainability incorporating a complex programme of initiatives that range from a green façade that can help cool and clean the building to programmatic elements including a network of canals and a lake at the base of the building for public use.

From simple, low-maintenance designs to more complex geomorphic approaches to architecture involving smart technologies and experimental new building materials, these visually seductive, and at the same time intelligent responses modify our relationship to water and open up the field of architecture to new solutions for achieving safer, healthier and more equitable modes of living.

Industry and Infrastructure

Since the late 19th century, the edge between the city and the water has been dominated by commercial and industrial structures that have cut off public access and provided eyesores of heavy industry, pollution and dense traffic. Up until the 1960s, waterfronts were largely ignored by the public and were more likely to be characterized by a high-speed roadway, like the stretch of highway that wraps Manhattan in New York City, than a distinctive element in a city's social, economic and physical life. Technological changes and a move towards a more service-oriented economy has moved much of the industrial activity out of the city and hence away from central waterfront locations over the last few decades. However, many necessary commercial buildings such as piers, ferry and cruise terminals or structures used by the coastguard remain a feature of the waterfronts, proving too costly or complicated to remove both logistically and ecologically. As waterfront renewal has taken seed in the last couple of decades as a way to enhance the urban economy and improve quality of life, historical vestiges of the waterfronts' industrial and manufacturing operations of the past prove both a challenge and an opportunity for the planning and management of cities in many parts of the world. As part of this resurgent interest in the waterfront, high-profile architecture is being used to upgrade these areas and introduce new uses and

Kansai International Airport, Osaka Bay, Japan,
Renzo Piano Building Workshop, 1994.

Ferry and Cruise Terminal, Hamburg, Will Alsop, 1993.

activities. As the American city planner Raymond W. Gastil has noted, "Open-minded societies design waterfronts that accept change, recognizing, in a deeply pragmatic way that all cities and all societies can be improved and thrive on continuous reinvention in their physical and critical expression." He adds that exceptional architecture and design is "seen as a world of cultural expression, integral to a city's growth – not marginalized as a bit of necessary decoration after the planners, finance committees and political actors have made all the decisions ..."[14]

One of the most stunning examples of new industrial waterfront architecture completed in recent years is Foreign Office Architects' Yokohama International Port Terminal that began operating in 2002. Designed by Alejandro Zaera Polo and Farshid Moussavi, principals of the London-based architecture studio, the multi-functional building has since been heralded for its innovative design. The project, which the firm won through an international design competition, called for a passenger cruise terminal with a mix of spaces for civic-led activities such as art exhibitions and sports areas. Rather than circulating traffic in a linear direction, FOA diagrammed a multi-directional space of unfolding surfaces that allows for interconnectivity between the various components of the pier, encouraging programmatic and public exchange. In addition, the multi-level site provides opportunities for physical and visual connections to be made between the water and the land, ensuring the project is read as a legible extension of the city.

FOA's design is comparable to other colossal projects built on water, with the notable example of Kansai International Airport, the first to be built on the sea, which includes a four-storey terminal designed by Renzo Piano Building Workshop. Opened in 1994, the complex comprises a mix of industrial and leisure facilities with recreational, retail and entertainment venues.

Smaller scale projects, however, can be equally powerful in providing new identities for industrial waterways. Will Alsop's Ferry and Cruise Terminal, constructed in Hamburg in 1993, proposes a new gateway to the city for passengers arriving by boat. The stepped façade of the glass and aluminum structure acts as a lookout tower over the water. Prefabricated parts made for an affordable building, constructed in a relatively short period of time. Gastil offers that "Alsop's ability to integrate a highly tectonic language with what can only be described as the experiential pleasures of architecture – decks stayed by thin cables, boarding through glazed tubes, an aggressive, memorable profile that has a technical and cultural relationship to its site – is unparalleled."[15]

Another project aiming to energize the waterfront is Waterstudio.nl's spectacular proposal for a Floating Cruise Terminal in Dubai, large enough to allow simultaneous mooring of three of world's largest cruise ships. The lifted point of the triangular shape forms the entrance to the inner harbour for smaller ships and water-taxis to mainland. Inside the terminal there will be 165,000 m² of space for retail, conference, cinema, hotel and similar uses.

Sarphatistraat office building, Amsterdam, the Netherlands, Steven Holl, 2000.

Concept proposal for a Floating Cruise Terminal for Dubai, United Arab Emirates, Waterstudio.nl, 2014.

Several designs that have a direct relationship with water were conceived by New York-based architect Steven Holl, including the Lake Whitney Water Treatment Plant discussed in this book. Resembling an extruded water droplet, the design of the building responds both physically and visually to its function as a water purification facility. Holl has also worked on the adaptive re-use of former industrial warehouses into new commercial and residential spaces, including the Sarphatistraat office building along the Singel Canal in Amsterdam. Surfaced in a mesh of plywood and copper, light pierces the multiple layers of the façade of this rectangular industrial building, changing its colour over the course of the day as a response to the changing nature of the adjacent waterway.

Waterfronts demand architecture that is unique in its interactive physical and programmatic engagement with the urban context such as the multi-level design for the Ponte Parodi in Genoa, Italy by Dutch architects UN Studio. The project functions both as a terminal for ferries and cruise ships and as a site for recreation and leisure facilities that extends the edge of the city out over the water.

The sculptural form of De Zwarte Hond's traffic control unit in the Netherlands is at once both a functional and visually aesthetic response to its waterfront setting that reinterprets previously designed industrial lookout towers.

Wave Garden is perhaps the most inventive project in terms of its environmental capabilities and hybrid functional components. Yusuke Obuchi conceived this progressive concept for a new type of landscape that combines a power plant and a recreational venue, while he was still a student of architecture

at Princeton University. Harnessing the potential of renewable energy sources, in this case, wave power, the project aims to make our energy consumption evident through physical elements in the landscape as a way to heighten our awareness of our natural resources.

1 Charles Landry, The Creative City: A Toolkit for Urban Innovators, London: Earthscan Publications, Ltd., 2000, p. 122.

2 Richard Marshall, Waterfronts in Post-Industrial Cities, London: Taylor & Francis, 2001, p. 54.

3 Ibid.

4 Denny Lee, "Bilbao, 10 Years Later", The New York Times, 23 September, 2007.

5 Charles Landry, The Creative City: A Toolkit for Urban Innovators, London: Earthscan Publications, Ltd., 2000, p. 123.

6 Tracy Metz, Fun! Leisure and the Landscape, Rotterdam: NAI Publishers, 2002, pp. 8-9.

7 Hans Venhuizen, ed., Amfibisch Wonen/Amphibious Living, Rotterdam: NAi Publishers, 2000, p. 17.

8 Ibid., p. 37.

9 James Wines, Green Architecture, Köln: Taschen, 2000, p. 56.

10 Ibid.

11 Julia A. B. Hegewald, Water Architecture in South Asia: A Study of Types, Development and Meanings Leiden: Brill, 2001, p. 196.

12 Ibid., p. 219.

13 James Wines, Green Architecture, Köln: Taschen, 2000, pp. 12-14.

14 Raymond W. Gastil, Beyond the Edge: New York's New Waterfront, New York: Princeton Architectural Press, 2002, p. 27.

15 Raymond W. Gastil, Beyond the Edge: New York's New Waterfront, New York: Princeton Architectural Press, 2002, p. 83.

Buildings and Projects
Lake | River | Sea

Floating House | MOS Architects

COMPLETION
2007

LOCATION
Lake Huron, Pointe au Baril, Ontario, Canada

DESIGN TEAM
Michael Meredith, Hilary Sample (design architects)
Fred Holt, Chad Burke, Forrest Fulton (project team)

CLIENT
Doug and Becca Worple

Commissioned to design a summer house on Lake Huron in Ontario, Canada, MOS Architects was faced with volatile tidal conditions in this exposed landscape. Their pragmatic solution resulted in a house that floats on a pontoon sitting on the water. Thus it can rise and fall with dramatic changes in water levels. Made from 2.4-metre-long and 1-metre-wide cylinders filled with air, the pontoon provided a stable structure on which to build a wood- and steel-framed house. "The pontoon was toed to the lake in good weather", explains Michael Meredith, who with his partner Hilary Sample directs MOS in Cambridge, Massachusetts. "We then had to wait until the winter when the water froze over and the pontoon was held in place to build on it. When the water thawed we toed the structure to its final site and did the final building work."

The house is part of a series of simple structures used as holiday homes on this remote island, which is located 3 1/2 hours north of Toronto and is accessed solely by boat. A pedestrian walkway links the houses together and creates a path across this natural landform. Ideally located in the middle of the U-shaped island, MOS' design creates a link between both sides of the island across the water, and is protected from changes in water levels generated by passing boats.

The floating house accommodates three bedrooms, a bathroom and a kitchen on the top floor as well as a sauna, two living rooms and a place to park a boat on the lower level. The house is tethered to the island via a wooden bridge that enters the house on the second floor and connects the building to the main public pathway. A deck on the far side of the house provides a sheltered play and relaxation space on the water and encloses a natural area for swimming.

The wooden slatted structure of the house was determined as much by environmental considerations as aesthetic decisions. The house is made from western red cedar wood, a material commonly used to make waterside docks, which is resistant to harsh weather conditions. The slatted structure frames the interior spaces. Where its density is more porous, wind can circulate and naturally cool the building, which has no other source of air conditioning – nor any heating. In addition, the slatted form filters the wind that pushes on the side of the house and helps keep the structure stable. Flexible hoses provide plumbing for the house and connect the building to the electricity grid. The upper level is enclosed by floor to ceiling glazed panels that provide views across the landscape.

Through the simplicity of form and building materials, MOS attempts to make as little visual and physical impact on the natural environment as possible and yet provides a visually elegant and functional summer house for weekend getaways on the Great Lakes.

The Floating House built on a pontoon on Lake Huron.

The Floating House is connected to the land by a wooden bridge that acts as the entrance to the building, providing access to the upper level of the house.

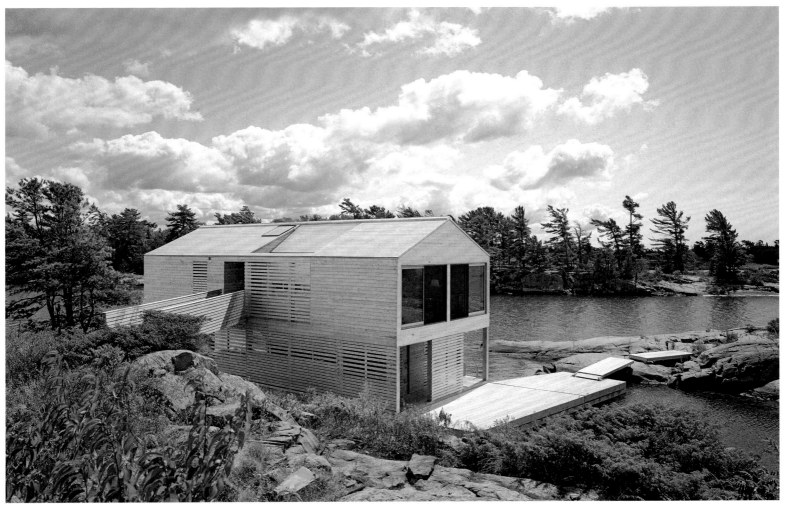

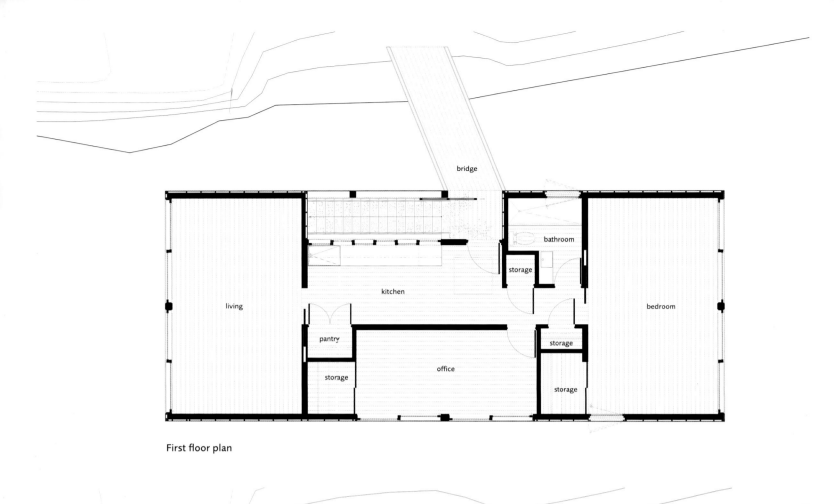

First floor plan

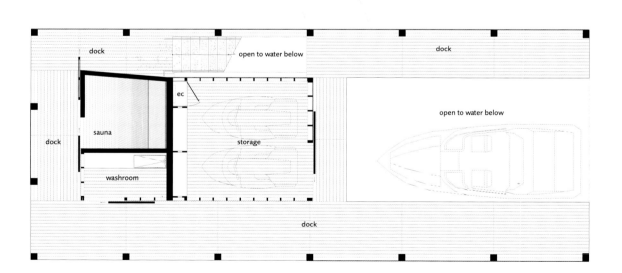

Ground floor plan

Night view of the Floating House.

Interior view of the upper level of the Floating House with panoramic views of the surrounding rural landscape.

Whitney Water Purification Facility
Steven Holl Architects

COMPLETION
2005

LOCATION
Lake Whitney, New Haven, Connecticut, USA

DESIGN TEAM
Steven Holl, Chris McVoy (design architects)
Anderson Lee, Urs Vogt (associates)
Arnault Biou, Annette Goderbauer (project architects)
Justin Korhammer, Linda Lee, Rong-hui Lin, Susi Sanchez (project team)

STRUCTURAL ENGINEERING
CH2M HILL; Tighe and Bond

LANDSCAPE DESIGN
Michael Van Valkenburgh Associates

CLIENT
South Central Connecticut Regional Water Authority

Most industrial plants do not typically inspire visits, but Steven Holl Architects' design for a water treatment facility in southern Connecticut doubles as a public park with educational tours where visitors can learn about water purification and conservation.

Given the importance of water as a natural resource, the design of the plant, which is situated on Lake Whitney, a natural reservoir, and which purifies up to 68,000 cubic metres of water a day for the state of Connecticut, takes into account its natural setting with a building that fuses the architecture with the landscape.

Light is often a driving element in Steven Holl's designs and water is embraced for its reflective properties and ability to connect architecture with the landscape. A case in point is the critically acclaimed Nelson-Atkins Museum in Kansas City, Missouri (2007), which is sited in front of a large pool designed in collaboration with artist Walter De Maria. Circular skylight discs in the bottom of the pool bring water-refracted light into the garage below.

In the Lake Whitney project, the architects decided to embed the majority of the water treatment below ground. Project architect Chris McVoy explains that, "Usually, for treatment plants like this, engineers build big boxes, and try to make it look like something with applied architecture. We proposed to put all the functions (seven-eighths of the total) below the ground under a new park." The challenge was then how to make visible the plant's workings and engage the general public. The result is two-fold based on both the architecture and the landscape component of the site.

The main visual element is a 110-metre-long extruded stainless steel tube that houses the plant's administrative facilities and public programmes. Like an inverted drop of water, the reflective property of the shiny surface of the building reflects the sky and natural surroundings connecting it to the land.

The decision to build below ground was as much aesthetically driven, allowing for the 5.7-hectare site park above, as it was pragmatic and environmental. Embedding the plant below ground sets the treatment process below lake level, allowing the water filtration to be gravity-driven, thus obviating the need for energy-consuming pumps. Every aspect of the building has been considered in terms of its environmental impact and sustainability. This includes using local materials wherever possible such as the cast concrete that makes up 40 percent of the overall building materials with cork and re-cycled glass-chip floor tiles used throughout. The plant has the largest green roof in Connecticut, spanning 2,790 square metres, increasing insulation and controlling stormwater run-off. Skylights that resemble water bubbles in the green roof bring light down into the plant and maximize connections between the two environments as

Aerial views of the Water Purification Facility showing its adjacency
to the Lake Whitney natural reservoir (upper right corner).

well as provide natural lighting to the areas below. McVoy states that taken together, "The below-grade location of the process spaces, the insulation value of the green roof, the thermal mass of the extensive concrete tanks and walls, and a ground-source heating and cooling system minimize the project's energy consumption."

The public park, designed by landscape architect Michael Van Valkenburgh from Cambridge, Massachusetts, is arranged in six sections, which are analogous to the six stages of the water treatment process. Developed in collaboration with the Connecticut Department of Environmental Protection, the US Army Corps of Engineers and the Inland Water Committee, a plan for extensive erosion control and water conservation was put in place. Stormwater runs naturally across the site and is filtered and cleaned through the six different landscapes, each inspired by the internal working of the plant processes: rapid mix, flocculation, air flotation, ozonation, granular activated carbon (GAC) filtration and a clear well. Landscaping rather than pipes circulate the stormwater into the treatment plant.

The park, a natural wetlands, caters to local residents as a recreational venue as well as to visitors to the neighbouring children's museum. Designed to demonstrate the water treatment process, it has also been reconstructed as a natural habitat for birds, insects and small mammals. McVoy assserts that from the beginning, the brief was manifold, and that the project should "educate the public about environmental issues, such as maintaining an abundant supply of clear water, protecting riparian resources, and encouraging sustainable wetlands stewardship." In addition to the on-site considerations, the plant also respects the needs of the adjacent Mill River, which is connected to the lake by a waterfall. In order that the flow of the river is not disrupted, only enough water to satisfy the needs of the region is extracted through a pipe that feeds into the water purification plant, maintaining the local ecology of the site.

The treatment plant exemplifies the possibilities of integrating industrial facilities with the natural environment in a way that establishes links between mechanical and natural process, both of which are essential to sustaining life.

The entrance building to the water purification plant resembles an extruded drop of water, a reference to the building's function.

top left: Overall view of the stainless steel tube housing the administrative and public facilities.

bottom left: Site plan.

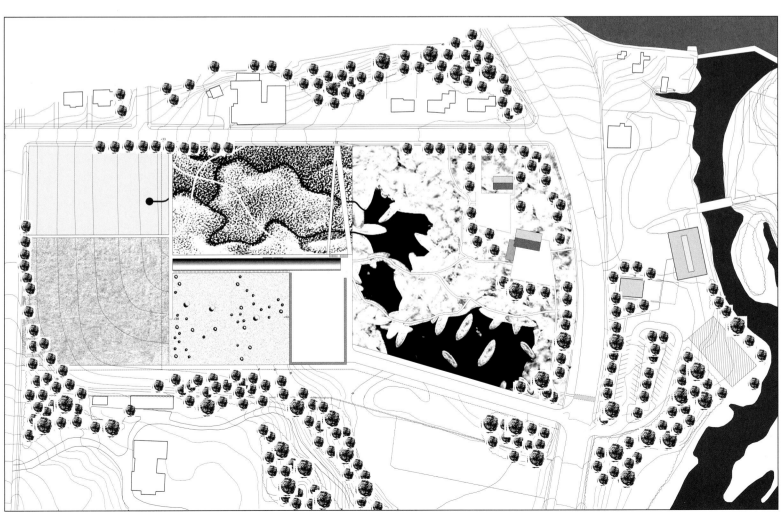

top left: View across the water to treatment plant.

bottom left: Colourful indigenous plants cover the green roof which contributes to the control of stormwater run-off.

The green roof over the water treatment plant is punctuated with skylights that bring light into the building.

Aluminium Forest | Abbink X de Haas Architectures

COMPLETION
2002

LOCATION
Houten, Utrecht, the Netherlands

DESIGN TEAM
Micha de Haas (partner)
Stephan Verkuijlen, Machiel Bakx (project team)

STRUCTURAL ENGINEERING
TNO-Bouw; D3BN Structural Engineers

CLIENT
Stichting Aluminium Centrum

Commissioned to design a new headquarters and display space for an aluminium company, the Dutch architecture firm Abbink X de Haas has originated a building that is a showcase in itself. Inspired by the belief of the father of fractal geometry, Benoit Mandelbrot, that to make something more simple you have to first make it more complex, the Aluminium Forest, as it has been dubbed, is the first building to be completely made with an aluminium load-bearing structure. 368 tubular columns ranging from 90 to 210 millimetres in diameter support a rectangular volume housing 880 square metres of floor area that is partly built on land and partly on water. Drawing reference from the polder-strewn landscape of the Netherlands, the building, which sits on stilts over an artificial lake in Houten, near Utrecht, has been made possible with technology developed by the aerospace industry and incorporates state-of-the-art energy efficiency systems. What makes it stand out, however, is the minimalist detailing, the "simple" part of this multi-faceted construction that belies the extensive research and development that was required to develop the special aluminium mullions that give the structure its elegant form.

Abbink X de Haas was established in 2008 when Architectenbureau Micha de Haas (founded in 1997) and Abbink Falk urban architecture (set up in 2002) joined forces. Based in Amsterdam, the practice is focused on design and research across the fields of architecture and urban design. Their work comprises a range of residential and mixed-use buildings for sites across Holland, in addition to a number of projects on water including a floating house and the interior design of a luxury houseboat for families living in Amsterdam.

The firm was approached by the Stichting Aluminium Centrum in 1999 to develop an eye-catching design that would illustrate their cutting edge practice and the properties of aluminium that make it a favourable building material: its lightness and strength. It is also 100 percent recyclable.

Building out over the water was as much an environmental decision as a pragmatic one. The above ground site gave the possibility for a larger floorplan but also enabled the design team to push the boundaries of building with aluminium extrusions. De Haas notes that, "The design breaks with the general assumption that aluminium is most suitable for façades and window-framing element and demonstrates its capacity and competence as a structural material." Custom-made profiles integrate window frames, insulation and the panels for the façade. The clip frame structure creates an airtight envelope. Sections are interchangeable and replaceable in case of damage. Other sustainable aspects carefully thought out by the design team include energy efficiency. Geothermal heating sourced from a pump drilled into the ground of the water reservoir is used for heating and cooling the building. De Haas asserts that it is exactly "this combination of poetic effect and technological innovation which gives this building its formal interest."

Night view of the Aluminium Forest built on stilts. The design was inspired by the typical Dutch polder landscape where groups of trees are planted in a square arrangement.

Detail view of the sleek aluminium-clad box of the Aluminium Forest building supported by an irregular arrangement of aluminium columns.

top right: By using aluminium, a material celebrated for its lightness and strength, the architects were able to raise the Aluminium Forest building above ground, affording panoramic views of the surrounding landscape.

bottom right: The aluminium columns both provide structural support for the building and act as drain pipes and service conduits to the building above.

An elevator and two aluminium staircases (that can be raised like a drawbridge sealing the building for security purposes) provide access to the building. The design of the interior is based on maximizing space and light. Offices and showrooms are arranged around a central stairwell and light shaft. Unobstructed sightlines through the building are made possible by open-plan rooms with views through cut-outs in the surface of the building that provide another source of natural light. Patios framed at the edge of the space also prompt a constant interplay between the inside and outside of the building.

The legs of the building, which give the project its name, are an irregular arrangement of poles raked at different angles just like the irregular trunks of trees growing in nature. The stilts help stabilize the volume and in addition maintain the visual relationship between the built structure and the surrounding waterscape.

View of internal staircase.

right: A glass elevator core provides access to an open-air public space on the upper level main floor of the building.

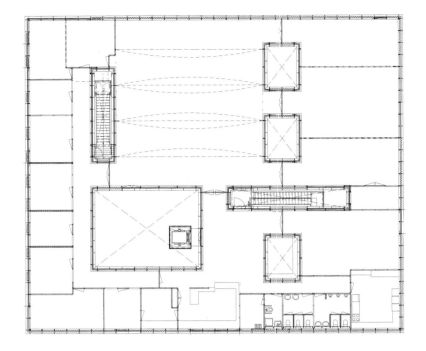

First floor plan

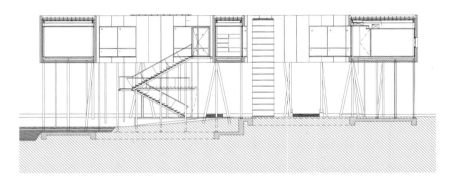

Section

Silodam | MVRDV

COMPLETION
2002

LOCATION
Amsterdam, the Netherlands

DESIGN TEAM
Winy Maas, Jacob van Rijs, Nathalie de Vries, Frans de Witte,
Eline Strijkers, Duzan Doepel, Bernd Felsinger

STRUCTURAL ENGINEERING
Cauberg Huygen

CLIENT
Rabo Vastgoed, De Principaal B.V.

For more than a decade, the Netherlands has been a rich source of inspiration for designers and architects working on revitalizing urban waterfront settings. Borneo Sporenburg, a residential community built to the north of Amsterdam in the Eastern Docklands in 2000 that accommodates 17,000 residential units has become a model for future regeneration projects on formerly abandoned industrial wastelands. Although not without controversy, the project, led by landscape architects West 8, sought to utilize a collaborative approach to achieve a diversity of modular living units built on two docks along Amsterdam's waterfront. Twelve architectural partnerships including Caroline Bos and Ben van Berkel of UN Studio, Kees Christiaanse of KCAP, and Willem Jan Neutelings of Neutelings Riedijk Architects were invited to design units which have since been praised for providing a diversity of living conditions and encouraging a mixed community of residents.

Silodam housing development in the western section of Amsterdam's former harbour is another housing block that has become a study in dense urban living. Like the Borneo Sporenburg development, Silodam is also sited along the IJ River in Amsterdam. It takes its name from two former grain silos, renovated and turned into housing, that are located in the area, which until the early 20th century functioned as a thriving industrial harbour. In the 1980s when the majority of the shipping industry relocated to the outskirts of the city, the municipality of Amsterdam began re-envisioning the area as a potential site for redevelopment taking advantage of the proximity to the water, the river views as well as its location near the urban centre.

Designed by the architectural office of MVRDV, the project encompasses 142 owner-occupied units, 15 rental units and 600 square metres of commercial space built on a 300-metre-long pier, and it responds to the need for live/work complexes that encourage a mix of uses.

MVRDV, known for innovative housing projects and the adaptive re-use of industrial buildings along waterfronts in various parts of the world, explain that the stacked design of Silodam originated as an effort to create a diverse range of "little neighbourhoods" that would give the housing block a unique character. Erected on concrete pillars, the complex offers patio apartments, studios, studio apartments, maisonettes and penthouses. The different types of apartments are differentiated by colour and material, from timber to brick. On the western side of the building a large terrace for use by all residents juts out over the river with a small mooring area for boats. At the base of the building on the ground floor are the office spaces. Below this is a terrace that runs the length of the pier and forms a broad quay at the front. Residents and visitors have access to both terraces where they can take in the water views. Tracy Metz, an architectural critic, commends MVRDV "for offering the water views to the public as

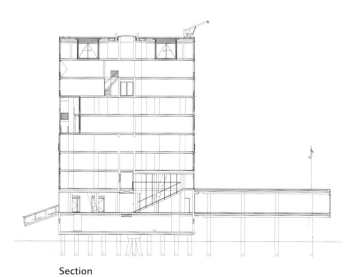

Section

The colourful stacked box arrangement of Silodam distinguishes it from other residential or commercial buildings on Amsterdam's waterfront.

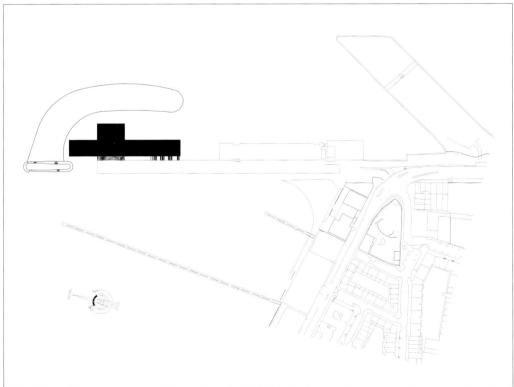

Site plan

well as residents. It's a thrill to see when you get up close that the building is actually built over the water, and that you can moor your boat directly under it." However, she also notes that, "As time has gone on, it turns out that there has been quite a turnover of residents", something she hopes will not be exacerbated in the future when new housing between the Central Station and Silodam along the IJ will offer more up-to-date living spaces.

Skepticism aside, Silodam exists as a unique and intelligent solution to the housing shortage in the Netherlands as well as one that takes advantage of its waterfront setting. It also offers a range of intelligent design solutions such as its parking system. A hydraulic lift delivers cars to a lot under the pier, ensuring the upper level is kept free for pedestrian activities. The colourful stacked composition of the building attracts the eye. The design, although drawing on its industrial heritage for inspiration, reinterprets this familiar language and thereby introduces a new type of residential architecture for the 21st century.

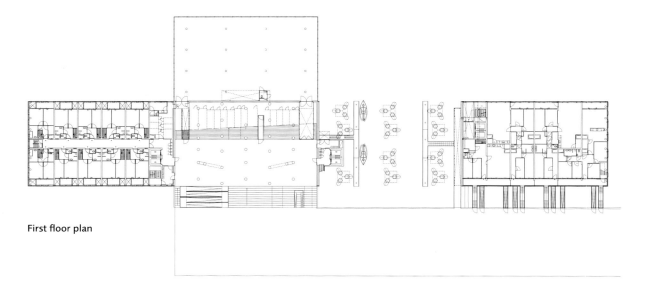

First floor plan

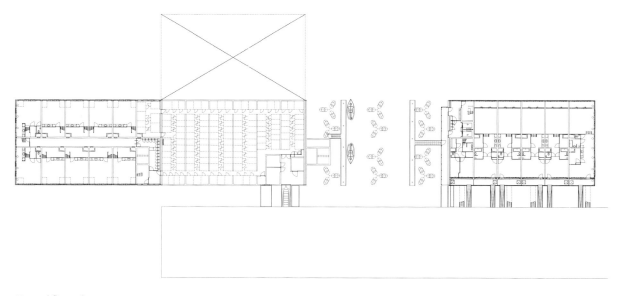

Ground floor plan

River façade with the large terrace jutting out over the river for use by all residents.

Detail view of the live/work spaces with the terrace deck.

Concrete pillars support the complex. Underneath the building there is a small mooring area for boats.

Maison Flottante | Erwan and Ronan Bouroullec

COMPLETION
2006

LOCATION
Paris, France

DESIGN TEAM
Denis Daversin (project architect)
Jean-Marie Finot (naval architect)

CLIENT
Public commission, CNEAI

Erwan and Ronan Bouroullec are known for their functional yet poetic furniture and product designs. More recently, however, they have expanded their oeuvre to include work at the scale of architecture. Lit Clos, from 2000, gave a hint of this new direction. The white and green metal sleeping loft suspended above ground on stilts is a cross between a bunk bed and a tree house. Produced by Italian manufacturer Capellini, the compact structure provides an autonomous sleeping and living compartment. Prior to this in 1998, Ronan Bouroullec designed Modular Kitchen, a customizable environment for preparing food, followed by Joyn Office, a modular workspace manufactured by Vitra in 2002.

Wanting to further exploit our relationships with space, the Bouroullec brothers have created a houseboat, a project that comes close to building design. The Maison Flottante (Floating House) was commissioned by the Centre National d'Edition d'Art Imprimé (National Centre for Printed Art), or CNEAI for short, as a residence for artists and authors invited by the centre to work on projects. The structure is tethered to the Île des Impressionnistes (Island of Impressionism), an island in the river Seine in western Paris. Sylvie Boulanger, Director of the CNEAI explains that they wanted "an architectural object not an architectural building that is fixed to the earth and permanent. The boat is a less permanent structure and open to interpretation by the artists." The choice of a houseboat was also the result of city planning regulations that do not permit building on the island. The 110-square-metre floating studio provides an autonomous space for artists to work in that is nonetheless supported by the adjacent art centre. The houseboat is made from an aluminium framework surfaced in wooden trellis that will be covered with foliage over time, providing an additional layer of privacy. It will also ensure the studio blends with its natural surroundings. The Bouroullec brothers, who worked on the project with celebrated naval architect Jean-Marie Finot, were selected because of their "capacity to design something that is simple yet elegant and practical", notes Boulanger and adds that "the minimal design belies its complexity given the waterfront site." The streamlined structure is outfitted with two bedrooms and a large studio space. Large doors open at either end on to outdoor terraces and allow for natural ventilation. Much of the work commissioned by artists for the centre is made from mixed media and is rarely made by a single artist but with co-authors, editors, software engineers, etc. Boulanger explains that the multiple room space and open structure is therefore "ideal for such collective work."

Maison Flottante, an artist's residence on the river Seine in Paris.

Night view of the Maison Flottante, a floating residence tethered to the land by a wooden and steel gangplank.

View of the simple, open plan interior of the Maison Flottante
designed to provide maximum connection between the inside
and the outside.

Night view of the Maison Flottante. The windows define different
live/work spaces book-ended by two open-air terraces.

right: View from inside the floating residence across the river Seine.

Traffic Control Centre | De Zwarte Hond

COMPLETION
2002

LOCATION
Nijmegen, the Netherlands

DESIGN TEAM
Wim Feith (project architect)
Jurjen van der Meer and Tjeerd Jellema (project team)

CLIENT
Ministry of Public Works & Water Management Building Agency

Traffic control units on waterfronts are more often than not inconspicuous and bland architectural structures and yet, as Dutch design team De Zwarte Hond has proven, they can be sculptural landmarks. Designed for the Rijkswaterstaat, the national public works and water management bureau in the Netherlands, the traffic control unit, built in 2002 near Nijmegen in eastern Holland, sits at the intersection between the river Waal and the Maas-Waal canal, one of the busiest shipping thoroughfares in the country. Charged with designing a look-out tower and administrative office that would provide the widest view possible over the water, the studio conceived of a sweeping three-storey volume that protrudes out over the water.

De Zwarte Hond is a multi-disciplinary design studio founded in 1985. Led by Jurjen van der Meer, Jeroen de Willigen, Willem Hein Schenk and Eric van Keulen, the firm's diversified team works across the spectrum of architecture projects from commercial to residential and institutional buildings, as well as landscape and urban design. Recent projects include an administrative building for Groningen University and a high-rise residential tower on the waterfront in Friesland, the Netherlands.

Key to their work is the importance of developing site-specific design solutions focused on the inherent social and cultural elements of a project. This mandate was the driving force behind the design of the control tower. Constructed from a concrete core, framed in steel and supported by a latticework of girders, the curved structure is clad in titanium panels. A wide slit through the centre of the structure, like a gaping mouth, provides unobstructed views across the water. A random pattern of narrow windows also pockmark the surface across all three floors.

The building is entered from the ground by an external staircase at the rear of the building and a ramp that slopes up over the beachfront, protecting workers from the water when the tide is high. The ramp, made from wood and Cor-Ten steel, divides halfway to forge two entrances: one to the control room on the second floor and another to the level below. The shiny titanium panels of the body of the building are in contrast to the rough surface of the ramp. De Zwarte Hond state that the design "could easily be mistaken for a simple metaphor for the maritime industry." However, they see the design as "a logical translation of a purely rational approach."

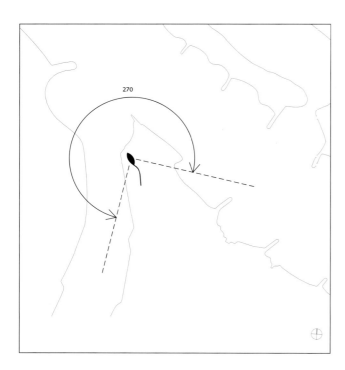

Site plan

top right: View across the water to the Traffic Control Unit showing its mouth-like look-out windows.

bottom right: View of the overland ramp that provides access to the Traffic Control Unit.

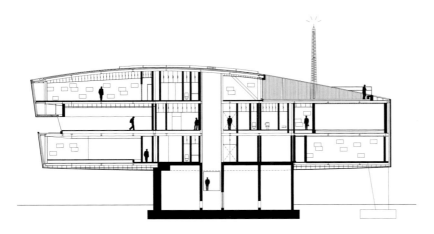

Section

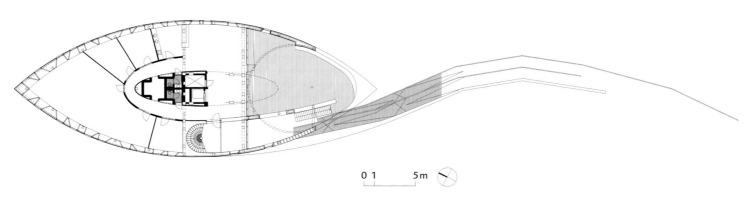

Second floor plan

0 1   5m

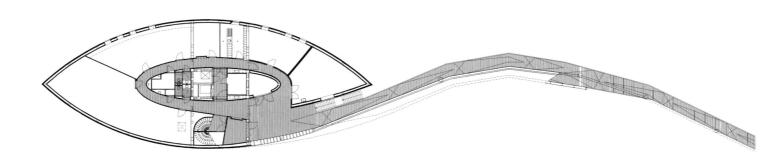

First floor plan

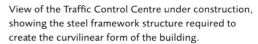

View of the Traffic Control Centre under construction, showing the steel framework structure required to create the curvilinear form of the building.

Entrance from the ramp.

View of the Traffic Control Centre with a passing boat.

Control centre interior.

View of the conference room.

Island in the Mur | Studio Acconci

COMPLETION
2003

LOCATION
Graz, Austria

DESIGN TEAM
Vito Acconci, Dario Nunez, Stephen Roe, Peter Dorsey, Thomas Siegl, Gia Wolff, Nana Wulffin, Laura Charlton, Sergio Prego

STRUCTURAL ENGINEERING
Zenkner & Handel; Kurt Kratzer

CLIENT
Graz 2003, Cultural Capital of Europe

Hearing Vito Acconci describe his design process often recalls images of a conjurer performing tricks or a contortionist bending and flexing his body in an unfathomable way. For example, for the design of the Island in the Mur, a cultural venue that is part theatre, café and playground, he explains that the design team started by looking at the conventional form of a theatre: a bowl. "We realized that if we twisted the bowl, if we turned the bowl upside-down, we'd have a dome: this would be the café, the roof of the café. The warping space from bowl to dome, and vice versa, would be the playground." In other words, "One space twists and turns and warps to become the other."

Vito Acconci, whose office Studio Acconci is based in Brooklyn, is most well known as an artist whose poetry, performances and videos from the 1960s and 1970s continues to be exhibited internationally. In the early 1980s, Acconci became interested in developing public works that invited viewer participation and reconsidered traditional architectural typologies. In 1992, he collaborated with architect Steven Holl on a new modular façade for Storefront for Art and Architecture in New York that doubled as seating and exhibition space. In 1998 he created "Flying Floors for Ticketing Pavilion", a series of sculptural resting areas for Terminal B/C at Philadelphia International Airport. More recent projects include a store for fashion designers United Bamboo in Tokyo and a sculptural entrance pavilion for the Canon Performing Arts Center in Memphis.

The Island in the Mur, commissioned by Graz 2003, Cultural Capital of Europe, floats on the river Mur in the heart of the city of Graz in Austria. Constructed from a latticework of 320 tonnes of steel and glass, the bulbous form of the island resembles a seashell and was determined by the need for the structure to allow for the flow of the river and to withstand possible floods. "The river is tidal, so our island had to rise and fall with the tide. We had to account for the 50-year flood, the 100-year flood. Our island had to ride the tide, surf with the tide", explains Acconci of the metaphorical starting point of the project. In addition to the formal components of the design, the flow of circulation between the spaces was also inspired by the context of the water. "Since we were designing a place on the water", acknowledges Acconci, "we wanted that place to be as fluid as water: we didn't want to get water out of our minds, we wanted to think as water …"

As well as a performance venue, the project forms a bridge across the river. Ramps lead down to the central outdoor amphitheatre, which also acts as a viewing platform over the city. Generated initially as a temporary project with a one-year life span, the pod-shaped performance venue proved so popular that it has become a permanent feature on the river.

left: Aerial view of the Island in the Mur, which is connected
to the urban fabric by bridges leading to either side of the river.

Night view of the Island in the Mur performance space.

The island houses an open-air amphitheatre.

Café interior.

Elbe Philharmonic Hall | Herzog & de Meuron

COMPLETION
2011

LOCATION
Hamburg, Germany

DESIGN TEAM
Jacques Herzog, Pierre de Meuron,
Ascan Mergenthaler, David Koch (partners)
Jürgen Johner, Nicholas Lyons, Stephan Wedrich (project architects)

STRUCTURAL ENGINEERING
Hohler + Partner Architekten und Ingenieure

CLIENT
Freie und Hansestadt Hamburg
represented by ReGe Hamburg Projekt-Realisierungsgesellschaft GmbH

The second largest city in Germany, Hamburg is the commercial and cultural centre of the northern part of the country and its harbour is second only to Rotterdam in Europe. Like so many cities it has long overlooked its waterfront as nothing more than an industrial wasteland suitable only for heavy trade. In the last decade, however, this underused area has experienced a rapid process of transformation. Known as HafenCity, this sprawling development lies between the historic Speicherstadt warehouse district and the river Elbe. The 155-hectare area, set for completion in 2020, is being reconstituted as a centre of culture and commerce that will increase the downtown area of Hamburg by 40 percent with a mix of office, retail, residential and cultural buildings.

In addition to a new science centre by the Dutch partnership Office for Metropolitan Architecture, a new home for Hamburg's NDR (North German Radio) Symphony Orchestra, designed by Swiss architects Herzog & de Meuron is planned as the cultural centrepiece of this urban improvement project.

The project necessitates the renovation of the brick warehouse Kaispeicher A, built by Werner Kallmorgen in 1963–1966. The architects call attention to the behemoth structure by crowning it with a trapezoidal-shaped crystalline structure that glows at night. The Basel-based design team headed by Jacques Herzog & Pierre de Meuron employ a similar strategy to that used for the Tate Modern, an adaptive renewal project that has become a beloved symbol of contemporary London. Their suggestion to leave the original power station building largely intact was in fact what helped them win the project. The Elbe Philharmonic similarly merges the old and the new in a dramatic new design that is ideally sited at the Sandtorhafen, the tip of the harbour that juts into the river. The public-private venture will also include a luxury hotel, residential apartments, conference centre, a wellness centre, the Klingendes Museum (a music museum for children), restaurants, bars, a nightclub and parking.

The most dramatic and visible part of the new design is the new public plaza that will be constructed on the top of the old warehouse and serve as the entrance to the various parts of the complex. Envisioned as a viewing platform and gathering space in the sky, it is sheltered from the elements by a large glass structure that perches on top. At night the glass volume will light up like the summit of a lighthouse, recalling the area's industrial past but signaling its future aspirations. The wave-like form of the crest of this striking edifice and its semi-transparent milky coloured finish is an obvious reference to the surrounding waterscape. However, the use of glass, cut open at points, provides a counterpoint to the solid brick base and opens the building up to views into and out of the structure, taking advantage of its auspicious location at the juncture of this historical waterway and the urban frame, and reflecting its new role as a public space for the city.

Rendering of the Elbe Philharmonic that includes the renovation of a formerly industrial warehouse crowned by a new crystalline structure that will house a concert hall and additional commercial facilities as well as public spaces.

View across the river Elbe to the Elbe Philharmonic.

top left: The Elbe Philharmonic under construction.

bottom left: The original warehouse Kaispeicher A, built in 1963–1966, prior to the conversion into the Elbe Philharmonic.

Rendering of the fluid interior spaces of the new crystalline structure.

Science Centre | OMA

COMPLETION
2008 (design)

LOCATION
Hamburg, Germany

DESIGN TEAM
Rem Koolhaas, Ellen van Loon (partners), Marc Paulin (project architect),
Mark Balzar, David Brown, Alexander Giarlis, Anne Menke, Sangwook
Park, Joao Ruivo, Richard Sharam, Anatoly Travin (project team)

STRUCTURAL ENGINEERING
Binnewies GmbH

CLIENT
G & P, ING Bank

In *Delirious New York: A Retroactive Manifesto for Manhattan*, Rem Koolhaas' seminal text published in 1978, he writes of the importance of water to the city's urban life, noting how "Those large arms of the sea which embrace Manhattan Island, render its situation, in regard to health and pleasure, as well as to convenience and commerce, peculiarly felicitous." His words remain relevant three decades later but could just as easily apply to a number of other cities in the world including Hamburg where Koolhaas' Office for Metropolitan Architecture (OMA) is currently working on a new flagship for the city's harbour which has abandoned its industrial heritage and is being reborn as a new recreational and cultural centre. The new premises for the Hamburg Science Centre is being billed as a striking entranceway to the city from the water, located at the end point of an urban axis from the inner Alster to the river Elbe.

In Hamburg, OMA are part of a wealth of talented designers that have been commissioned to contribute to the 155-hectare HafenCity dockland development. The grandiose scale and ambitious programme of this new structure match the commanding nature of the vast harbour area. The pixilated form of the Science Centre, which is 72 metres high at its peak, is realized through a stack of ten irregular-shaped boxes shifted off axis like children's Lego bricks. The number ten responds to the different programmatic elements that make up this 275,000-square-metre cultural campus that will be home to a science centre, a science theatre and an aquarium built below ground level. Marc Paulin, the project architect, explains that "The form is the product of programme by circulation", referring to their architectural design strategy that enabled them to define the form and layout of the building based on its programmatic functions and a desire for a legible and cohesive circulation system throughout the building. "We wanted to create a building that would connect both sides of the Magdeburger Harbour", affirms Paulin, "rather than create a building that would back onto the water and therefore block visual and physical access to the water." By excavating a 40-metre-wide hole at the centre of the building, sightlines through the structure from the water and the city are made possible. In addition, the building acts as a bridge with numerous points of access for pedestrians via cuts in the building out to the water's edge. The modular form of stacked boxes, inspired by shipping containers, was determined early on in the design process as a flexible system that could be customized as needed. The driving concept was the interweaving of advance research in science with the exhibitions on display. The continuous looped form of the building aims to avoid the banality of many conventional skyscrapers that Paulin notes typically "accommodate merely routine activity, arranged according to predictable patterns. Formally, their expressions of verticality have proven to stunt the imagination: as verticality soars, creativity crashes."

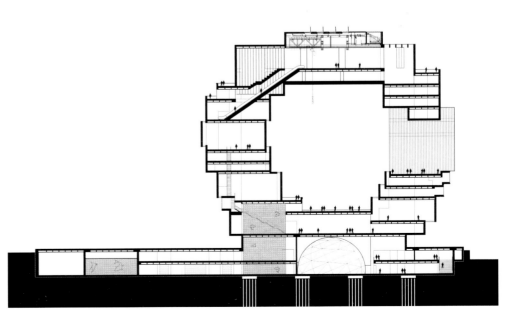

left: The design for the new Hamburg Science Centre will be constructed from a series of boxes stacked on top of one another in a circle.

The pixilated structure next to a multi-storey cruise ship.

Hamburg Science Centre in the context of the city and its waterfront.

Section.

Ponte Parodi | UN Studio

COMPLETION
2009 (design)

LOCATION
Genoa, Italy

DESIGN TEAM
Ben van Berkel, Caroline Bos with Astrid Piber, Nuno Almeida and Cristina Bolis, Paolo Bassetto, Alice Gramigna, Michaela Tomaselli, Peter Trummer, Tobias Wallisser, Olga Vazquez-Ruano, Ergian Alberg, Stephan Miller, George Young, Jorge Pereira, Mónica Pacheco, Tanja Koch, Ton van den Berg Advisors

STRUCTURAL ENGINEERING
Arup, London

CLIENT
Porto Antico, Altarea

UN Studio, led by Ben van Berkel and Caroline Bos and based in Rotterdam, rose to prominence in 1996 with their most important waterfront project, the design of the Erasmus Bridge in Rotterdam. Nicknamed "the swan" by locals because of its elegant form poised over the river Maas, the cable-stay bridge links the northern and southern halves of the city with a 790-metre span.

The three-dimensional planning of space is at the heart of a new waterfront project to convert a 19th-century pier in Genoa, Italy, into a terminal for ferries and cruise ships with recreation and leisure facilities that will encourage a bustling vibrant environment beyond that generated by the transportation hub. The multi-level design for the Ponte Parodi was inspired by Venice's Piazza San Marco, which has long been an attraction for locals and visitors alike, drawn to its cafés as much as to its history and culture. For their piazza on the water, UN Studio were charged with creating a meeting point that enjoys similar performative qualities and mixes of activities, drawing people from the city centre to the water 24 hours a day. "People are central to the effect of the piazza", assert the designers. "We need to plan around people and their movements in order to create an active location."

From the water, the pier looks like an artificial hill that echoes the undulating landscape of Genoa rising behind. The multi-tiered design is made up of a web of interlocking spaces that allows for a constant physical and visual exchange. The project defines what UN Studio call their "kaleidoscopic" approach to architecture, which grows out of a tendency to develop complex geometries of form in which the ground, wall and ceiling are manipulated into continuous spatial experiences that create fluid environments seamlessly integrating various programmatic features.

The design of the 80,000-square-metre site began as a cube that has been pulled apart to accommodate the various functions. The extruded form is punctured with diamond-shaped cuts in the surface that organize the vertical circulation and provide sightlines through the spaces on the pier down to the quay on the west side where cruise ships dock. The diamond cuts also act as shafts for natural light to penetrate lower levels. Sited at the peak of the pier is a multi-level public park for recreation. Look-out points across this sculpted landscape connect to terraces that slope down to the lower levels where spaces for culture as well as offices and sports facilities are located. The programmatic aspects of the site are clustered together according to a time-based strategy that takes into account the attractiveness of times of the day and the waterfront setting. The designers assert that cafés, retail outlets and dining facilities are organized by where the sun rises and sets. Therefore, "Coffee can be taken in the morning sun with a view towards the sea; midday shopping offers shadow and evenings are spent watching the sunset." UN Studio's approach results in site-specific designs that offer an infinite series of surfaces and spaces, encouraging appropriation by diverse communities.

left: Site plan of Ponte Parodi in the context of Genoa harbour.

A circulation diagram illustrating the points of connection and access between the new recreational and commercial venue and the city and harbour.

Section.

Ground floor plan showing the multi-tiered landscaped terraces that define the top surface of the Ponte Parodi for use as recreational public spaces.

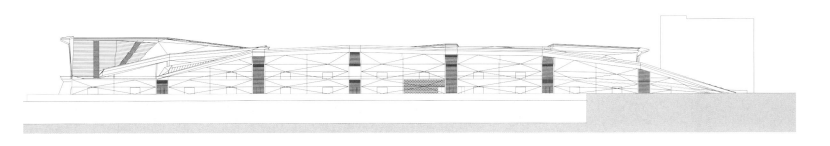

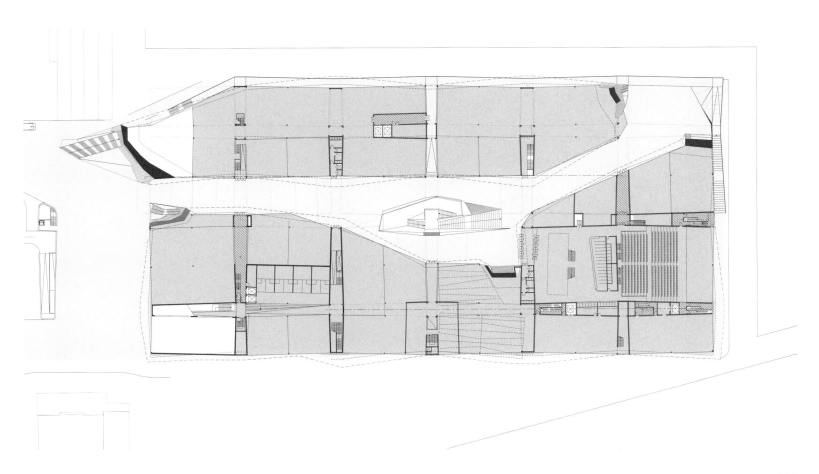

Harbour Bath | BIG and JDS Architects

COMPLETION
2003

LOCATION
Copenhagen, Denmark

DESIGN TEAM
Bjarke Ingels (project architect), Julien de Smedt (collaborator),
Finn Nørkjær (project leader), Jakob Møller (project architect),
Christian Finderup, Henning Stüben, Ingrid Serritslev, Marc Jay (contri-
butors), CC Design (wooden platform consultants)

CLIENT
The Municipality of Copenhagen

In 2006, Adrian White, an analytic social psychologist at the Universi-ty of Leicester's School of Psychology, analyzed data published by a range of venerable sources including UNESCO and the New Econo-mics to create a global projection of subjective well-being. The result: Denmark is the happiest place in the world, based on a combination of high standards of health, welfare and education. One possible reason for this is the enormous investment the country makes in its public spaces to encourage social interaction, relaxation and play, in an effort to increase quality of life. The Harbour Bath, a bathing and recreational space in the centre of Copenhagen, is one such project. The result of a national competition organized by the city, the perma-nent recreational venue on the water was designed by Bjarke Ingels of Bjarke Ingels Group (BIG) and Julien de Smedt of JDS Architects, formerly principals of the now disbanded studio PLOT.

Since the 1980s, the city government has led an initiative to transform the formerly industrial harbour into a cleaner, more environmentally friendly mixed-use district. Limiting commercial shipping traffic in the inner harbour, relocating factories away from the water, and reducing the amount of wastewater entering the harbour through stormwater overflows have had wide-reaching positive consequences for the har-bour and its return to public use. At the same time, developers and planners have teamed up to revitalize the adjacent Brygge Islands with new residential and recreational functions such as the Harbour Bath. Situated along the old shipping dock, the project is in many ways the culmination of these efforts, offering Copenhageners the opportunity to bathe in newly clean seawater while also serving as a dynamic extension of the new Harbour Park.

The artificially created landmass accommodates 600 people daily with pools for swimming and landing areas for sunbathing and gatherings. The design is essentially an elegant wooden deck that extends from the land. It accommodates three pools that span out in radial lines from the centre of the lifeguard station that is positioned at the high-est point of the decking, giving the lifeguards unobstructed views across the bath from all angles. A shallow pool that gradually slopes to a depth of 0.6 metres for use primarily by children and the elderly generates a beachfront-like setting for play activities and relaxation. A second pool of 1.2 metres in depth was envisioned for older child-ren and ball games. The third and largest pool is 86 metres long and 8 metres wide for use as a lap pool. The entire facility is accessible via a ramp and each pool has been made accessible for people of all abilities. For the designers, the solution is as simple as "reinterpreting the water... by adding land."

To date, the Harbour Bath continues to teem with people during the summer months. Its success is due both to its inviting design and the city's insightful approach to urban planning that gives high priority to urban renewal projects that benefit the population at large.

Wooden decks frame the pools at Harbour Bath in Copenhagen, Denmark.

Aerial view of the Harbour Bath within its urban context.

Circulation diagram, showing also the multiple access points for disabled patrons.

top right: Detail view of the diving platform (on left) and look-out tower (on right).

bottom right: The Harbour Bath in use.

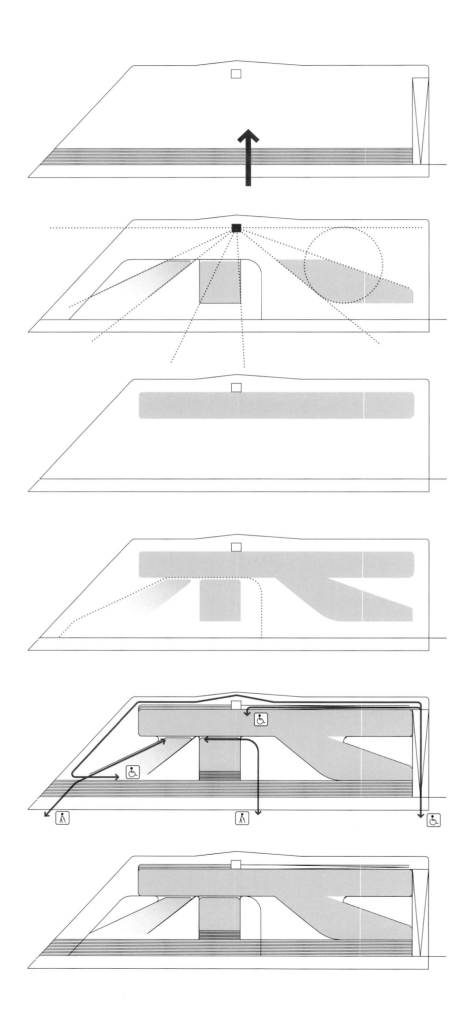

Kastrup Sea Bath | White Architects

COMPLETION
2005

LOCATION
Kastrup, Denmark

DESIGN TEAM
Fredrik Pettersson (project architect), Rasmus Skaarup, Pernille Vermund, Göran Wihl, Henrik Haremst, Johnny Gere (project team)

STRUCTURAL ENGINEERING
NIRAS Rådgivende ingeniører og Planlæggere A/S

CONTRACTOR
Tårnby commune

"My idea was to achieve a sculptural, dynamic form that can be seen from the land, from the sea and from the air. The silhouette changes as the spectator moves around it", says Fredrik Pettersson of the sweeping form of the Kastrup Sea Bath near Copenhagen, completed in 2005. A cross between a recreational pier and a lido, this contemporary open-air pool encourages swimming in an area protected by a wooden windbreaker. Located off the coast of Amager, a Danish island in the Øresund, partially inhabited by the nation's capital city, Copenhagen, the Kastrup Sea Bath is set within a beach area to the east of the island. Since its inception in the 1930s, the Amager Strandpark (Amager Beach Park) had fallen into disrepair. The Kastrup Sea Bath was envisioned as a centrepiece of extensive redevelopment of this area, which took place between May 2004 and August 2005.

White Architects, with eleven offices across Scandinavia, is known for their work which ranges from architecture and urban planning to landscaping and interior design. They are dedicated to identifying solutions focused on issues of environmental and ecological sustainability through material research and the employment of new technologies in the construction and building management process. Current projects include the New Karolinska Solna, a university hospital building in Stockholm, Sweden, and a range of nature centres for the Swedish Environmental Protection Agency.

Led by architect Fredrik Pettersson, the design of the 750-square-metre wooden sea bath creates a sheltered platform out on the water for recreational activities. Made from azobé wood, chosen for its durability, the curved structure is elevated above the water on stilts. The load-bearing structure is visible below the wooden platform, as in a traditional pier. The organic form of the bathing pier is an extension of the beach and culminates in a 5-metre-high diving platform. Complete with changing rooms and areas for sunbathing, the circular bathing area is also equipped with stepped terraces and benches made from wooden planks that provide space for individuals and groups to relax and congregate. In the winter the pier is still accessible and acts as a viewing platform over the water. LED spotlights and floodlights illuminate the inside of the structure at dusk. A simple wooden 90-square-metre building adjacent to the sea bath on the beachfront provides services for beach-goers.

After many years of abandonment, Kastrup's beachfront is now a welcome recreation spot for people of all ages intrigued by Pettersson's design, which to him rises from the sea "like an impressive sea-monster", albeit a friendly one!

Detail view of Kastrup Sea Bath in relation to the nearby beachfront.

right: View of Kastrup Sea Bath from the beach, showing the sweeping form of the boardwalk.

top left: View of the elevated ramp that provides access to Kastrup Sea Bath.

bottom left: Detail view of the stepped surfaces of the boardwalk at Kastrup Sea Bath, which provide different surfaces for use by bathers.

Kastrup Sea Bath in use.

East Beach Café | Heatherwick Studio

COMPLETION
2007

LOCATION
Littlehampton, West Sussex, Great Britain

DESIGN TEAM
Thomas Heatherwick (design)
Peter Ayres (project architect)
Fred Manson (project associate)

STRUCTURAL ENGINEERING
Adams Kara Taylor

CLIENT
Brownfield Catering

British designer Thomas Heatherwick is known for his commanding sculptural designs. His studio works to push the boundaries of materials and production processes in an effort to create powerful creative expressions. Heatherwick founded his now 50-person-strong studio in 1994 after graduating with degrees in three-dimensional design from Manchester Polytechnic and the Royal College of Art in London. His interests lie in the confluence of art, science, engineering and design as exemplified by his portfolio of work that includes a rolling bridge, which coils up elegantly into a complete circle using hydraulic rams, and the urban renewal of a public space in Manchester known as the Blue Carpet due to its surface of blue glass tiles. Most recently he was selected to design the UK Pavilion at the Shanghai Expo in 2010 with a design that will have an interactive skin that can be programmed to project images, colours and messages.

His first architectural work to date, however, opened in 2007. Although a relatively small project, the East Beach Café in Littlehampton on the southeast coast of England is proving a popular destination for locals and visitors alike who are drawn not only to the much-praised menu but also to the curvilinear design that mimics the waves of the sea. Jane Wood and her daughter Sophie, the proprietors of the café, obtained planning permission for the design in 2005, which replaces a non-descript kiosk that was originally on the site.

The starting point for the design was determined by the context of the narrow site, set between the sea and a row of houses behind. Rather than the typical white-washed clapboard structures with striped awnings that characterize many of the seaside cafés along the English coast, Heatherwick explains that, "The studio saw its challenge as being to produce a long, thin building without plane two-dimensional façades."

Heatherwick achieved this by surfacing the building in ribbons of Cor-Ten steel that take on a rust-like patina when weathered. Like the hard shell of a crustacean, the steel frames and protects the cave-like interior space. The dining area can seat 80 with waiter-service and a further 60 diners can be accommodated outside on the terrace catered by a take-out menu. A glazed façade provides unobstructed views out to sea at the front. Shutters concealed within the geometry of the building can be rolled down to seal the building at night. The East Beach Café innovatively rethinks traditional types of eateries found along the English coast and raises the bar for seaside dining.

left: The East Beach Café on the beach at Littlehampton, UK

Detail view of the crustacean-like outer shell of the café, which derived from its coastal setting.

Interior view of the café.

Rear view of the volume's sculptural form.

Performing Arts Centre | Zaha Hadid Architects

COMPLETION
2008 (design)

LOCATION
Abu Dhabi, United Arab Emirates

ARCHITECT
Zaha Hadid and Patrik Schumacher (design), Nils-Peter Fischer (project director), Britta Knobel, Daniel Widrig (project architects), Jeandonne Schiijlen, Melike Altisinik, Arnoldo Rabago, Zhi Wang, Rojia Forouhar, Jaime Serra Chamoun, Philipp Vogt, Rafael Portillo (project team)

STRUCTURAL ENGINEERING
AMPC Anne Minors Performance Consultants (theatre),
London Sound Space Design / Bob Essert (acoustics)

CLIENT
The Tourism Development and Investment Company of Abu Dhabi (TDIC)

Zaha Hadid, the Iraqi-born, London-based architect, is well known internationally for her designs that suggest speed and flight through their sculptural forms that contour across the landscape. The expression of movement and the flow of activity are essential aspects of the Abu Dhabi Performing Arts Centre. Sitting at the end of the main axis slicing through Saadiyat Island, a natural, large, low-lying island 500 metres off the coast of Abu Dhabi Island, the project juts out over the Persian Gulf.

Saadiyat Island is a large budget project accomodating a number of signature cultural buildings, including an outpost of the Guggenheim museum, designed by Frank Gehry, a dependance of the Louvre by Jean Nouvel Studios, a maritime museum by Tadao Ando and the Sheikh Zayed National Museum by Foster + Partners.

Nils-Peter Fischer, the project director for the new Performing Arts Centre explains its design in kinetic terms: "We wanted to create momentum for the main axis through the city by generating a design that provides an intersection between the National Museum, which sits at the centre of the island, and the waterfront. The building is a water feature visually connected to the water."

In plan, the sculpted form of the building resembles a plant that has erupted from the ground and opened out like a flower in bloom at its apex, 62 metres above the ground. The structural elements of the building, a continuous flow of concrete arms, delineate the different levels of this multi-tiered structure. They also frame the glazed façade, which is crisscrossed by a mesh of trusses reminiscent of the veins in a leaf. Carved out of the inside of the building are five auditoria of which the concert hall on the top has the most dramatic relationship to the surrounding environment. Each venue is separated from one another by individual foyers connected by a central space bathed in natural light from skylights above. "We wanted to create a marketplace-like situation that has an urban feel", asserts Fischer of this space which has been carefully defined as a portal for concert goers and others alike.

The bulk of the building sits out on the water. The directional gesture of the building out to the sea exploits its setting. Narrow conduits of water have been pulled in on either side, bridged by a series of overpasses that provide pedestrian access to these waterways. These inland channels are protected from the strong tidal conditions of the Gulf by an artificial sea wall. Currently, the island, which lies on a foundation of sand, is undergoing extensive engineering efforts to counter sedimentation and erosion. In addition, the island is being modelled and re-landscaped to create the artificial profile needed for future construction efforts.

Concept rendering of the Abu Dhabi Performing Arts Centre, designed to jut out over the water.

Aerial view of the distinctive plant-like form.

Night view showing the vein-like pattern of the glass and concrete façade of the building.

Main auditorium with panoramic views of the water.

Institute of Contemporary Art
Diller Scofidio + Renfro

COMPLETION
2006

LOCATION
Boston, Massachusetts, USA

DESIGN TEAM
Elizabeth Diller, Ricardo Scofidio, Charles Renfro (principals), Flavio Stigliano (project leader). Deane Simpson, Jesse Saylor, Eric Howeler (project team)
Perry Dean Rogers and Partners (associate architects), Martha Pilgreer (principal), Gregory C. Burchard, Mike Waters (project manager), Henry Scollard (project designer)

STRUCTURAL ENGINEERING
Arup New York, Markus Schulte

CLIENT
ICA Boston

"All of the architectural gestures respond to the condition of being on the water", asserts architect Charles Renfro. Working with partners Elizabeth Diller and Ricardo Scofidio of New York-based architecture studio Diller Scofidio + Renfro, Renfro explains that their design is anchored by its waterfront location, "either through abstracting the image of water or providing particularized views to the waterway, an active shipping channel." The best overviews of the building are in fact from the water where one can get an understanding of the building's design in its entirety. The new home for this more than 70-year-old arts centre broke ground in 2004 after the site was dedicated for civic use by the Chicago-based Pritzker family, sponsors of the prestigious Pritzker Architecture Prize and owners of the Fan Pier properties along the Boston Harbour.

Renfro asserts that the waterfront location proposed a blank slate for the architects. "It had no existing structures and little industrial past" compared to other post-industrial waterfront sites in America. The project, the first building designed by the practice from the ground up, presented an opportunity to reconsider the traditional white cube typology of contemporary arts centres and introduce a building that is an original creative expression inspired by the urban context of this waterfront site.

Over the past 20 years Boston has been engaged in city-wide regeneration projects; the first art museum to be built in Boston in almost 100 years. It is envisioned as the cultural linchpin of a wider redevelopment of the Fan Pier harbour district. Plans, still to be realized, include residences, commercial and civic buildings, and a hotel complex, which will surround the museum creating a compact new area of the city.

The ICA is as much about the interior spaces as it is the design of the public spaces around the building and at the waterfront. The building provides triple the space of the old museum which was located in a former police station. There are offices, a restaurant and outdoor eating areas, a bookstore and a two-storey education centre with workshops. Understanding the need for flexible environments that can change to accommodate different types of artworks, they have designed a 19,800-square-metre, four-storey visual and performing arts centre made up of a variety of spaces that can house a range of artworks and spaces for contemplation. The glass-fronted design has been likened to a giant periscope or lighthouse, when illuminated at night. What these associations speak to is the building's open face, which not only provides views out on to the city but also allows those outside the building to look in on activities and programmes.

The designers describe the building as a "valve", through which they filter views through the gallery spaces and out onto the harbourfront. Entering the building on the south side, visitors ascend to the top floor in a glass-walled, room-sized elevator with views across the

View of the main entrance.

water. Two windowless galleries return the gaze into the interior of the museum and to the works on display. Filtered light enters through a fabric gauze-covered ceiling that can be blacked out when needed. The Founders Gallery to the north edge of the top floor opens up views to the outside via floor to ceiling windows. Suspended below the top floor is the Mediatheque, an enclosed, stepped out space with views of the water, which houses a digital media centre. Below this, on the floor below, is the 1,600-square-metre indoor performance space. Its glazed façade can be blacked out if needed but when open allows passers-by to view performances inside.

The most dramatic part of the design is the 5,000-square-metre top floor, the largest level of the building, which is cantilevered over the main bulk of the building, out over the HarbourWalk at the water's edge. DS+R was able to achieve this significant gesture by brokering a deal with the Boston Redevelopment Authority that allowed them to retract the footprint of the building to the north in order to widen the HarbourWalk in front in exchange for the right to overhang the coastal path. The luminous 24-metre-long box is kept aloft by four trusses of 7 metres in depth.

The boardwalk unfolds to create a dramatic staircase that rises to the first floor of the building. Made from the same wooden planks as the boardwalk, this public viewing platform and gathering place is seamlessly integrated into the harbour front. As Renfro explains, "The wood shears and spills into the building first as an exterior grandstand then as interior theatre stage and seating area and finally inverting overhead to form the ceiling of the theatre and the ceiling of a new exterior room on the edge of the harbour." This spatial element was important to the design team as a method of symbolizing "the public-ness of the building and at the same time literally forming the public spaces of the building." This elegant design strategy increases the feeling of connection between the inside and outside of the building.

DS+R explain their architectural solution as a conscious effort to strike a balance between the more formal interior spaces in the building such as the galleries, theatre and educational facilities, and the expansive exterior spaces at the water and around the building that have yet to be fully defined by the redevelopment plans. "We were interested in the building making a new kind of public space", notes Renfro, "one that feels in many ways interior due to the large cantilevered galleries overhead, and domestic, due to the use of wood planking." However, the architects point out that the public space at the front of the building will only be fully legible when the developments around the museum take ground. In addition, public transportation connections are necessary to connect the building to the city, including realization of a ferry stop planned for immediately west of the ICA's front door which will help make the museum a destination people will keep revisiting.

125

The ICA's glass façade provides continuously unobstructed views over the water.

Gallery space.

top right: Night view of the ICA Boston illustrating its prominent position on the waterfront. The building has been designed so that all major axes lead to the waterfront, reinforcing the integral relationship between the building and its site.

bottom right: Lateral view at night. The upper floors are glazed with frosted glass so that they glow like a light box from within. The effect is similar to a lighthouse when viewed across the water.

National Opera House | Snøhetta

COMPLETION
2008

LOCATION
Oslo, Norway

DESIGN TEAM
Kjetil Trædal Thorsen, Tarald Lundevall, Craig Dykers, Sigrun Aunan, Simon Ewings, Rune Grasdal, Tom Holtmann, Elaine Molinar, Kari Stensrød, Øystein Tveter, Anne-Cecilie Haug, Ibrahim El Hayawan, Tine Heg i, Jette Hopp, Zenul Khan, Frank Kristiansen, Cecilia Landmark, Camilla Moneta, Aase Kari Mortensen, Frank Nodland, Andreas Nygaard, Michael Pedersen, Harriet Rikheim, Margit Tidemann Ruud, Marianne Sætre, Knut Tronstad, Tae Young Yoon, Ragnhild Momrak, Andreas Nypan, Bjørg Aabø, Chr stina Sletner

STRUCTURAL ENGINEERING
Reinertsen Engireering

CLIENT
Statsbygg – The Directorate of Public Construction and Property

The Nobel Peace Centre, designed by London-based architect David Adjaye, opened in 2005. The Deichmanske Library and Stenersen Museum, planned to open in 2012, was designed by New York-based REX in collaboration with the Oslo-based architects Space Group who are also developing the former industrial port into a new 1.8 million-square-metre mixed-use neighbourhood. A new ski jump at Holmenkollen is to be designed by JDS Architects. These are just some of the projects changing the architectural landscape of Oslo, Norway. Probably the most anticipated project, however, was the National Opera House that opened in 2008. The building has been referred to as a cross between an iceberg and a cruise liner. The vision of local architects Snøhetta, the more than € 430 million, 120-square-metre performing arts centre owes much of the expectation to its soaring design that appears to erupt from the fjord. Openness and accessibility were key concepts in the design that sweeps up from the water and results in a strikingly angular structure ramped over with a public space that is accessible 24 hours a day. Craig Dykers, principal of Snøhetta, describes that their intention was "to create a direct link between the urban context and the natural condition of the fjord. Rather than building a barrier or hard edge to the sea, the building ramps gently into and up from the water making it possible to actually engage directly with the water."

The project is made possible by a city-wide initiative begun in the late 1980s to clean the harbour and purify the water by removing industrial cargo from the water's edge to the outskirts of the city in an effort to reduce the amount of wastewater entering the fjord and to also reduce traffic in the city. Dykers explains that there have already been signs of improvement. "The new opera house has stabilized the pollutants on the seabed, making it possible for life to return to the area. On the opening day of the building, two swans appeared at the ramp's edge. Bird life was rarely seen before this cleanup took place." It is hoped that within five years of adjacent projects being completed such as a nearby roadway tunnel, it will once again be possible to swim in this part of Oslo's fjord. Similar projects in other Scandinavian cities such as Copenhagen have proven already that it is possible to transform formerly industrial harbours into sustainable public spaces that re-envision a new public life for the city.

Aerial view of the Oslo National Opera House within the context of the city and its harbour district.

top right: The stepped terraces around the building are a much-used public space.

bottom right: The glass façade of the Oslo National Opera House allows visitors to the site a glimpse of the attractive interior.

Snøhetta won the international design competition for the country's first national opera house in 2000. The building, which houses the Norwegian Opera and National Ballet companies, spans over five floors. Workshops for educational programmes, rehearsal rooms, changing rooms, storage areas, offices and additional back of house facilities are mostly concealed under the sloping roof, in addition to two auditoria designed in a classical horseshoe plan, which can seat 1,350 and 400 people respectively.

With the opera house, Snøhetta revisited earlier schemes such as their dramatic design for the 240,000-square-metre Alexandria Library in Egypt that like the opera house has an overt relationship to its surroundings. The 38,000-square-metre sloping white stone roof of the opera house functions as a public space for both performance-goers and non-ticket holders taking in the view. "People feel a natural connection to something they can walk on in the open, public realm", asserts Dykers. "By placing what many consider to be an elitist institution, an opera house, under the feet of the visitor, it changes one's connection to the place. It becomes more informal, more a part of one's life."

The building has purposely been opened up to function as the main gathering space in this part of the city, which is undergoing revitalization as a new live/work community with retail, residential and office buildings. The surface of the opera house is landscaped with a series of stepped terraces that encourage ease of passage over the building. Glass-fronted towers rises from the centre of the ramped space, providing glimpses into the cultural centre below and encouraging interactivity between the inside and outside of the space.

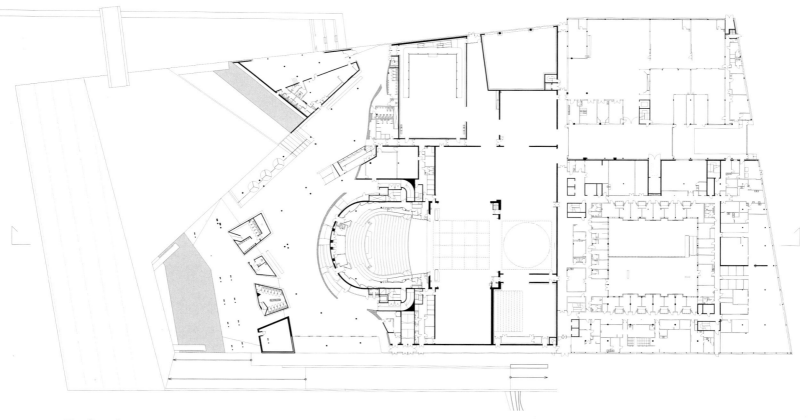

First floor plan

The glass façade of the Oslo National Opera House provides views across the harbour.

View of the main circulation spaces. A system of elevated ramps take patrons into the central auditorium.

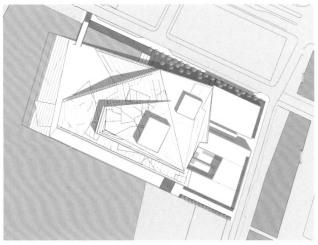

The white marble surface of the ramped roofscape of the Oslo National Opera House rises from the fjord like an iceberg.

Site plan showing the tiered roofscape.

To achieve the inherent relationship between the building and its waterfront location, Snøhetta worked closely with the Norwegian Maritime Museum on research into the environmental conditions of the site, a former industrial dockside. The site is protected by a 12,000-square-metre wall of steel sheeting that circumnavigates the perimeter of the site below the water level as a barrier against water seepage. The foundations of the building are supported by 28,000 metres of pilings reaching up to 55 metres below the water surface that are driven into stable bedrock. The polluted soil of this brownfield site, historically an industrial port terminal, is contained using geo-sheets (layers of man-made materials) that ensure that no toxic materials are distributed into the fjord. In addition, a 70-metre-wide barrier placed 2 metres below sea level has been put into place to prevent ships, which dock only 100 metres from the new building from colliding with the base of the opera house under water. Small leisure boats are permitted to dock along the side of the opera house.

The construction of the building has not escaped contention. At a soft launch in August 2006, which gave the public a glimpse of the building, three visitors suffered injuries when they tripped on the hard surface. In addition, some critics argue that Norwegian granite should have been used instead of Italian marble to cover the opera's exterior since the building aims to be a showcase of Norwegian architecture. This was emphasized when the marble appeared to yellow due to a chemical reaction to water. However, scientists claim that there are methods for drying out the stone that will restore it to its original colour.

However, putting these problems aside, the building has proven a popular attraction. On opening day, 30,000 people were welcomed to the site. "For many years engineers, developers and planners have used waterfronts to contain vast infrastructural systems as a matter of convenience for growth. While this was helpful, the effect is that most waterfronts have been entirely disconnected from the cities that surround them", explains Dykers. "The new opera house promotes an architectural and cultural identity that is both urban and natural. Its main plaza directly connects the sea to the sky via the form of a building. Also because the building is low to the ground it promotes connectivity rather than creating a wall between the city centre and the surrounding city."

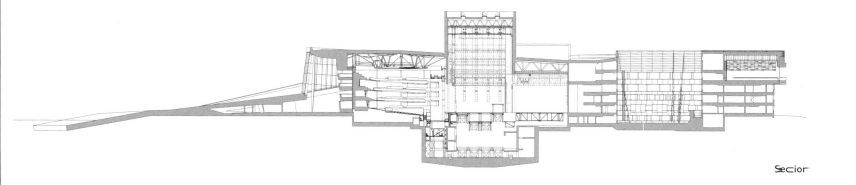

Section

Aerial view of the Oslo National Opera House within the context of the harbour.

View from the highway entering the city. The road which currently separates the opera from the city will be moved underground into a tunnel by 2013.

Opera House | Henning Larsen Architects

COMPLETION
2005

LOCATION
Copenhagen, Denmark

DESIGN TEAM
Henning Larsen, Peer Teglgaard Jeppesen (design)
Helle Basse Larsen, Anders Park (project architects)
Andreas Olrik, Carsten Hyldebrandt, Claus Simonsen, Dominic Balm-
forth, Finn Laursen, Hans Amos Christensen, Hans Vogel, Henrik Vuust,
Ina Borup Sørensen, Ingela Larsson, Jacob Nørløv, Jan Besiakov, Klavs
Holm Madsen, Klaus Troldborg, Krisztina Vago, Leif Andersen, Line
Lange, Lise Bækhøj, Mads Bjørn Hansen, Maria Sommer, Matthias Lehr,
Merete Alder Juul, Mette Landorph, Mette Lorentzen, Michael Bech,
Niels Brockenhuus-Schack, Nina Nolting, Osbjørn Jacobsen, Solveig
Nielsen, Søren Lambertsen, Søren Øllgaard Pedersen, Torsten Wang,
Trine Matthiesen, Troels S. Jakobsen, Troels Troelsen, Vibeke Lydolph
Lindblad (project team)

STRUCTURAL ENGINEERING
Ramboll Danmark A/S; Buro Happold

CLIENT
A. P. Møller and Chastine Mc-Kinney Møller Foundation

Danish architect Henning Larsen's largest work to date, the Copenhagen Opera House is sited along the historical axis that runs through
the centre of the city, starting with the Church of Our Lady, the national cathedral of Denmark, through to the Amalienborg Palace
square and the four royal residences. The 41,000-square-metre performance venue, that cost more than € 600 million, was designed as
the centrepiece of the harbour. Located on the former Royal Naval
Dockyard, the Opera House shares the area with 17th-century red
brick warehouses and barracks that now house the Royal Academy schools, which specialize in drama, film, architecture and music. The soaring 32-metre-long cantilevered roof and the colossal
sandstone, glass and steel form of the structure is visible from across
the city. Housed inside is a 1,400-seat auditorium, a 200-seat studio, numerous rehearsal rooms for orchestras, choirs, singers and
ballet dancers, workshop facilities, dressing rooms, costume shops,
administrative offices, a café, a restaurant that can accommodate 200
people, and several bars.

There is no denying the water references in the building's design.
Resembling a cruise ship in form, the bay-fronted four-storey foyer
is clad in glass with horizontal steel bands. Angled to look out across
the central harbour, the Opera House faces the Amalienborg, the
Royal residence. Part of a major project to redevelop the city's industrial waterfront with new residential, commercial and institutional
buildings, it commands attention.

Building on the waterfront is not a simple undertaking. The foundations for the building lie 14 metres under the water tethered to a steel
plate anchored to the seabed another 14 metres below that. The
basement level of the Opera House is constructed from a 1-metre-
thick concrete wall that can resist water pressure.

The hulking form of the Opera House is fronted by a plaza that is
sheltered by a stainless steel canopy framed in aluminium that cantilevers out over the public space. The overhang becomes increasingly
important as a physical and visual framing device when the plaza is
activated by impromptu events and activities as well as performances
organized by the theatre. The local plan for this part of Copenhagen
demands a public walkway along the waterfront, and the new plaza
is supposed to be a public space connected to it. As architect Helle
Basse Larsen explains, the plaza helps generate activity not only in
the evenings, when performances are taking place, but also during
the day. "People can visit the café at the Opera House or, when the
buildings on both sides are built, the shops and restaurants on the
ground floor of these buildings. The plaza is the point of connection
to the city", tying together the promenade that runs the perimeter
of the harbour.

Night view of the Opera House Copenhagen from across the harbour.

External view. The cantilevered roof hangs over the public spaces on the waterfront, creating a visual and physical connection between the building and the water.

top right: A look-out deck on the upper levels of the building provides panoramic views over the city.

bottom right: The construction of the Opera House Copenhagen has prompted new property development in the surrounding neighbourhood.

In addition to visiting the Opera House on foot, the building is also accessed by car from the city side of the building and by boat from the water. A small public ferry docks at the site each hour. To date, only the Danish Queen has docked at the Opera House by private boat.

The architects also worked on the master plan for the areas adjacent to the Opera House. At either side of the building, 17-metre-wide canals have been dug, accentuating the opera's position on an island. A series of bridges connect the site with the rest of the city. Low-rise apartment buildings and small business units are planned for the adjacent areas as well as the renovation and re-use of the historic warehouses that characterize this formerly industrial area. Basse Larsen hopes that the new plan will "create a city atmosphere that resembles the Christianshavn", a popular live/work neighbourhood to the southeast of the city centre dating from the 17th century and built on an artificial island, accessed by a series of bridges.

In contrast to the dramatic glass frontage of the Opera House, which rises five floors above ground, providing unobstructed views into the lobby and social spaces of the building, the rear side of the building is quieter in design. Sloping down to four floors in height, the sandstone façade in a range of muted hues is intended to blend in with the character of the new developments planned for this area. The bulk of the structure is striated with windows and narrow light slots. The top two floors are encased with glass to accentuate the effect of the floating roof element that sweeps out over the harbourfront.

The design of the foyer of the building is dictated by the bulbous form of the auditorium that juts out into the glass-fronted multi-tiered space. Its conch-like form responds to the acoustic needs of the building. Clad in dark stained maple wood, the curvilinear wall is the resounding feature of this airy space. Catwalk bridges connect performance goers to the upper balconies of the auditorium, providing limitless views across the space and out onto the water. Recessed lights dispersed throughout the space and three light sculptures by Olafur Eliasson illuminate the foyer at night to dramatic effect, particularly when viewed from across the water. As Basse Larsen asserts, the conch shell provided the inspiration they needed. "Its smooth surface and magic room inside where the sound comes from is exactly like the auditorium of the Opera House", she says. "It too houses wonderful music."

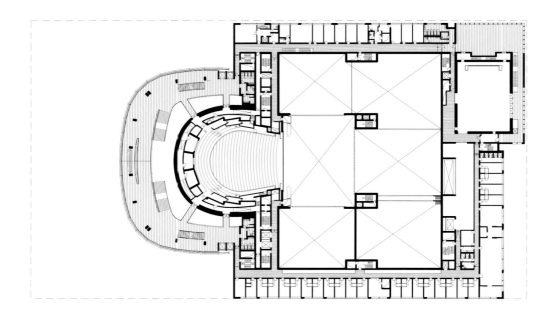

First floor plan

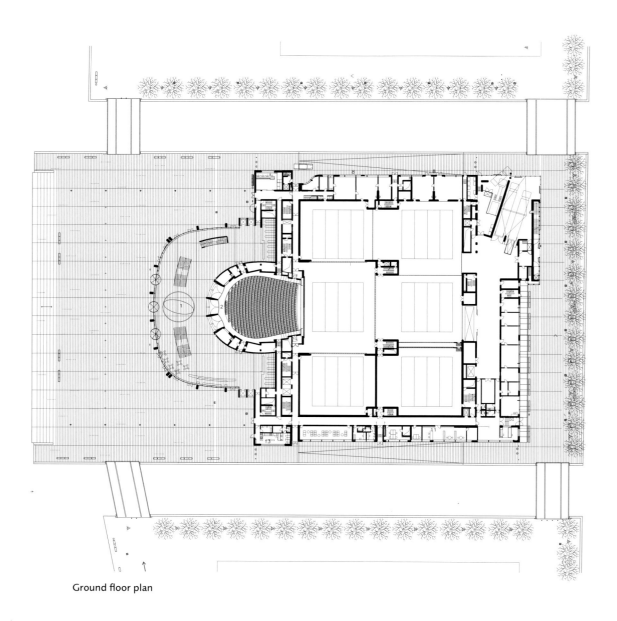

Ground floor plan

The interior provides views towards the harbour.

A pedestrian bridge provides access to the building.

Seoul Commune 2026 | MASS Studies

COMPLETION
2006 (design)

LOCATION
Apgujongdong, Seoul, South Korea

DESIGN TEAM
Minsuk Cho, Kisu Park (design), Joungwon Lee, Kiwoong Ko, Joonhee Lee, Bumhyun Chun, Dongchul Yang, Daewoong Kim, Jieun Lee, Jongseo Kim, Byungkyun Kim, Soonpyo Lee, Songmin Lee, Jisoo Kim (project team)

STRUCTURAL ENGINEERING
Teo Structure

CLIENT
Exhibition "Open House: Architecture and Technology for Intelligent Living", Vitra Design Museum, Weil am Rhein, and Art Center College of Design, Pasadena

Minsuk Cho's concept for Seoul Commune 2026, as its name suggests, proposes a new type of residential community that reconciles high-rise living with public space, promoting interactivity, healthy living and sustainability. Responding to the city's major housing developments over the past 40 years, Cho asserts that the projects that have survived and are viable today are in areas that "are complex in terms of their programmatic and social functions." In other words, they are areas in which a range of activities, people and spaces come together fostering interaction, exchange and social cohesion. Based on this premise, Seoul Commune attempts to replicate this concept vertically in a set of towers that provide private dwelling units and public space for community activities above ground, set within a green landscape. Cho explains that this project reflects a future direction for Seoul based on current demographic and societal needs. "We took the idea of the house as a single autonomous entity and translated that into a model that is closer to the structure of a city. This better reflects how we live today, especially in this region of Asia", where one or two person households are common. Added to an increasingly aging population and the rapid and widespread adoption of mobile technologies, Cho foresees a change in the types of homes people will require and in their mode of using these spaces.

The project was commissioned as part of "Open House: Architecture and Technology for Intelligent Living", an exhibition organized in 2007 by the Art Center College of Design in Pasadena, California, and the Vitra Design Museum in Germany that looked at how we might live in the future. Key to Cho's innovative design is water. A series of canals surrounding the towers connected to the adjacent river Han are an integral component of the design supplying energy and a latent cooling system that have been integrated into the scheme. This localized power supply reduces the project's need to rely on the city's chief power supply, generated by the West Sea more than 100 kilometres away.

Cho's towers-in-the-park concept derives its initial inspiration from such architects as Le Corbusier who in the 20th century envisioned the modern industrial city laced with highways, airstrips, and monumental towers surrounded by parks. Cho's vision is no less exciting but his concept updates such urban plans with a 21st-century mindset centred on creating living conditions that more readily respond to human needs and take into consideration the importance of environmental solutions to mega-scale building projects.

Cho founded his architectural firm MASS Studies in 2003 after a more than ten-year stint in the United States. Graduating with a masters in architecture from Columbia University in 1992, he founded Cho Slade Architecture with James Slade with whom he worked on projects in the US and Korea before returning to Seoul to set up his own practice. In 2000, Cho and Slade won the Architectural League of New York's Young Architects Award for their collaborative projects,

This series of residential towers called Seoul Commune provide – as the name suggests – both communal spaces and private residences covered in a latticework of foliage (fed with greywater from the towers) that would help to counter the environmental impact of the building. A series of canals connected to the adjacent river Han would create a latent cooling system for the structures.

The proposal includes 15 different types of towers each made up of an elongated classical plinth-like form with domes, inverted domes and inverted cone-shaped spatial structures located at different levels and at the top. Each tower provides a unique array of spatial configurations to suit different living conditions.

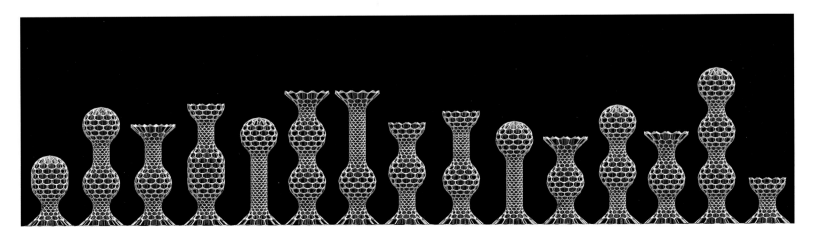

Aerial view of the proposed site on the river Han that will provide a dense system of new high-rise living as a response to Seoul's increasing need for single family residences.

The site transformed by the foliage-covered towers that would blend into the parkland.

Six diagrams illustrating the nexus of towers in the proposed Seoul Commune and the connections they will form with the site, the waterfront and the urban frame.

which range from housing in the US and Korea to a flagship store in Seoul for fashion designer Martine Sitbon and a children's theme park, home to Dalkhi, the Korean version of the popular Japanese cartoon character Hello Kitty. More recently Cho has worked independently on proposals for an extension to the City Hall in Seoul, as well as a number of commercial projects including most recently a new outpost for fashion designer Ann Demeulemeester with a façade made from herbaceous perennials that form what Cho describes as a "living wall". It is this radical concept that Cho proposes for Seoul Commune at an urban scale.

The 15 towers that make up Cho's new complex are each comprised of an elongated classical plinth-like form with domes, inverted domes and inverted cone-shaped spatial structures located at different levels and at the top of each. Cho proposes wrapping the towers in an external skin made from "geotextiles", a latticework structure covered in foliage and topped with a double helix structure that will help counter the environmental impact of the building. Greywater is filtered through a distribution system feeding the vines, which provide shade during the summer months. The green mesh is also embedded with a fog machine with automatic temperature and humidity sensors, which optimize the environmental conditions of the plants. This ecological system is responsible for 30 percent of the cooling load for the building in tandem with the geothermal cooling and heating system drawn from the nearby river Han. Photovoltaic panels on exposed surfaces of the building also increase energy efficiency.

Inside Seoul Commune private space is minimized in favour of communal spaces that promote social interaction and exchange. There are six variations of units with bedrooms and bathrooms. Living spaces are located on the exterior of the private units and shared among inhabitants. Cho equates the living quarters with hotel rooms, asserting that his vision calls for "each basic residential unit to satisfy private spatial needs, while the hotel's public space is shared and utilized by all, guests and non-guests alike."

The buildings are clustered together and linked at the base through a series of pedestrian pathways. Vehicular traffic is buried beneath ground. Pathways between buildings and a monorail on the second level provide connections between the communal spaces. One of the main aspects of the building is its location surrounded by canals and with a lake at its centre. As well as providing areas for recreational activities such as boating and swimming, the water sources are also part of the environmental strategy for the building, for example to enhance the latent heating and cooling mechanism of the building.

Cho concludes that although he accepts the model of large-scale urban development proposed by city planners such as Robert Moses in the United States, his design intends to couple this with the types of neighbourhood qualities – density and a mix of uses to encourage interactivity by a range of people – favoured by architectural critic Jane Jacobs. "By adding a rich programmatic and social complexity to the project we have created a new type of architectural typology that is truly urban and more fitting for 21st century living."

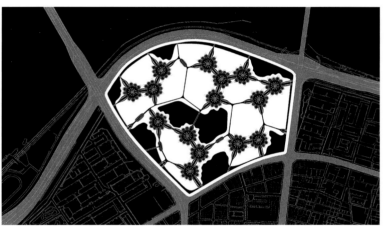
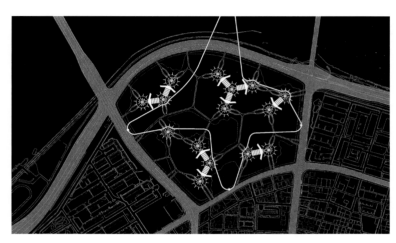
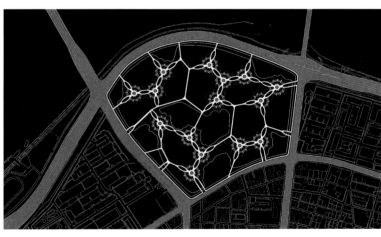
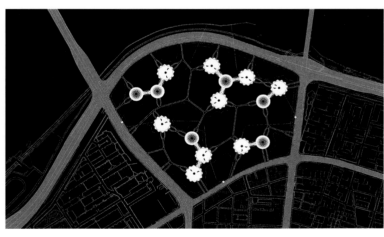
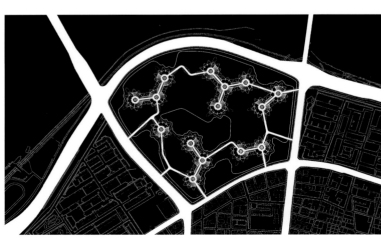
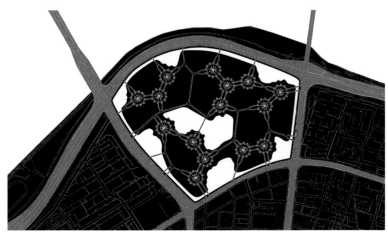

Jellyfish House | IwamotoScott Architecture

COMPLETION
2006 (design)

LOCATION
Treasure Island, San Francisco, California, USA

DESIGN TEAM
Lisa Iwamoto, Craig Scott, Tim Brager, Andrew Clemenza, Vivian Hsu, Ivan Valin, Leo Henke, Chris Gee, Tim Bragan, Eri Sano; Sean Ahlquist, Jason Cheng

STRUCTURAL ENGINEERING
Martin Bechthold

CLIENT
Exhibition "Open House: Architecture and Technology for Intelligent Living", Vitra Design Museum, Weil am Rhein, and Art Center College of Design, Pasadena

Exterior view of the proposed Jellyfish House, a concept for residential living that relies on digital technology. The outer skin of the building mutates in response to changing environmental conditions.

The open-ended structure of the Jellyfish House surfaced in glass provides unobstructed views across the landscape.

Smart homes of the past have typically focused on interconnectivity and the streamlining and speeding up of everyday activities through the use of state-of-the-art technology. The All-Electric House at the Johnson County Museum of History on display in the mid 1950s presented visitors with a glimpse into the future of modern technology with hidden televisions and electric curtain openers. The Monsanto House of the Future (1957–1967), an attraction at Disneyland in Anaheim, California, was a pod-shaped dwelling that offered insights into modern appliances such as the dishwasher, the microwave and an intercom system. Now living in a world that has surpassed the technologies included in these examples, Disney has teamed up with Microsoft, Hewlett Packard and LifeWare to develop an updated Home of the Future. Opened in the summer of 2008, the house explores the possibilities of a hyper-connected future with new home automation and automatic networking systems, touch-based computing and smart appliances.

Aside from the capabilities of new technology to enhance our social and cultural life, a host of architects, designers and others are experimenting with new visions for smart homes centred around environmental approaches that aim to transform the architecture of our homes from the inside and out.

The Jellyfish House, designed by San Francisco-based IwamotoScott Architecture, led by Lisa Iwamoto and Craig Scott, investigates the use of "calm technology", a branch of research associated with ubiquitous computing. Of concern to the architects is the level of interaction that much new technology demands of the user in the realization of the advanced architectural or interior elements in new model homes. They assert that "Interaction keeps something distant and other ... [and] requires that we centre our attention on the activity, like reading email or inputting cell phone numbers." Instead they suggest that digital and material technologies employed as a distributed network throughout a building engage "both the centre and periphery of our attention, allowing us to move fluidly between the two."

IwamotoScott's design was developed as a commission for the exhibition "Open House: Architecture and Technology for Intelligent Living", initiated by the Art Center College of Design in Pasadena, California, and the Vitra Design Museum, which challenged designers to develop new prototype housing solutions for the next 25–50 years that incorporate emerging technologies. Their design, as its name suggests, is inspired by a jellyfish. Like this sophisticated sea creature which has no brain, central nervous system or eyes, their building is highly adaptive to changing aquaculture. Iwamoto Scott claim that their design "Attempts to incorporate emerging material and digital technologies in a reflexive, environmentally contingent manner."

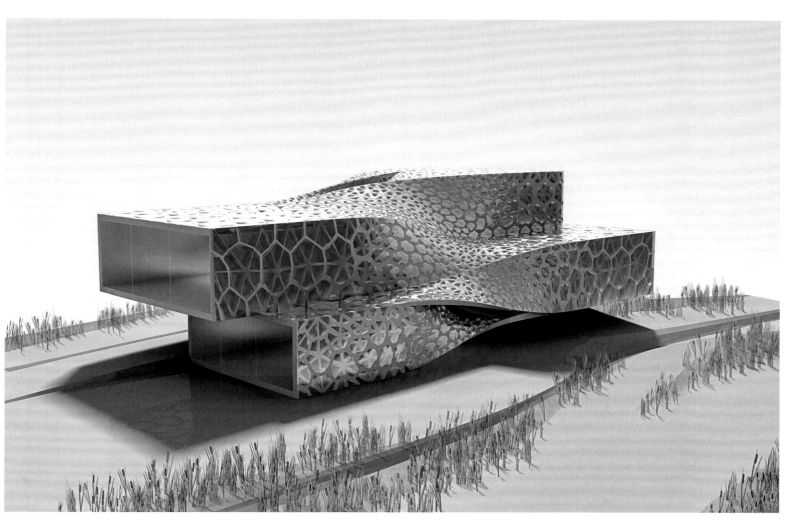

Detail view of the fluid spatial interior of the Jellyfish House.

top right: Although right angles are used in the design of the Jellyfish House to help determine different zones of activity, a series of ramps weave in and out of the house promoting a continuous flow of living spaces within the residence.

bottom right: Openings cut into the sides of the Jellyfish House provide continuous views to the surrounding landscape, ensuring physical and visual connections between the residence and its site.

IwamotoScott predict that in the future we will be able to inhabit formerly polluted areas in homes that will clean up their sites through water reclamation. The "Jellyfish House" was designed as a case study for this concept on Treasure Island, an artificial island and a former naval base in the San Francisco Bay between San Francisco and Oakland, connected to the wetlands of Yerba Buena Island. The two-storey building, made up of two open-ended tubes that twist together with a fluid spatial interior, responds to the condition of this brownfield site, its waterfront locale and additional environmental conditions such as wind, fog and the tides of the bay. IwamotoScott's interest lies in exploring how the introduction of an amphibious urbanism might treat this toxic ground by a process of water filtration. Their proposed strategy involves embedding into the island sinuous fields of wetlands that will remediate the toxins in the land and act as a natural filtration plant for stormwater run-off.

The Jellyfish house taps into this urban strategy through its mutable skin. Made from a parametric mesh that uses efficient geometric logic such as Delaunay triangulation, the cellular skin is designed to harvest and treat both rainwater and the building's wastewater. Water is first filtered through the veins of the façade, then passes through cavities in the walls and is exposed to ultraviolet light filaments, powered by thin film photovoltaics on the skin's surface that purify the water. IwamotoScott note that their design is realizable in the near future because the technology that it is based on is already commonly used at larger scales to kill micro-organisms and purify water. "Rather than having a PDA where you could control the house, it would be much more ambient", says Iwamoto. The cavities in the surface are coated in titanium dioxide, which absorbs the otherwise harmful UV rays, allowing only the blue, visible light to emerge. This results in the softly glowing structure that makes visible this cleansing process on the inside and outside of the house. The building is also responsive to light and weather conditions. Its skin is constantly fluctuating from opaque to transparent based on its layered construction and as water passes through its vein-like internal organization. However, the building's façade can be made entirely opaque if necessary. As Scott explains, "Not everyone wants to see inside the walls or be at the mercy of the outside at all times. They might want the walls to be more static so it is intended that users can intervene and shut down the changing state of the building."

The Jellyfish House builds on earlier case studies for smart homes such as Buckminster Fuller's ideas for his proposed Dymaxion House designed in 1927, which incorporated a greywater system. IwamotoScott integrate a latent heating and cooling system into their house through the use of phase change materials that either release or absorb energy as necessary. The designers state that although at present this type of heating and cooling system requires substantial changes in temperature, they predict that within the next 25–50 years the degree difference will be controllable to maintain comfortable temperatures within buildings. Like Fuller's, their project aims high. Let's hope this time, however, it becomes a reality.

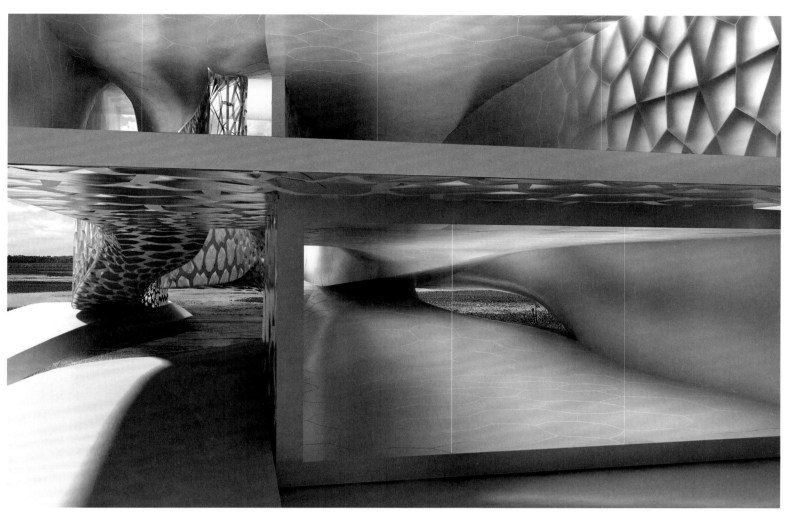

Wave Garden | Yusuke Obuchi

COMPLETION
2002 (design)

LOCATION
Southern California, USA

DESIGN TEAM
Yusuke Obuchi

CLIENT
Master thesis, Princeton University

The Wave Garden is a prototype for a new type of power plant, to be located just off the coast of southern California. Developed by Yusuke Obuchi as his master's thesis presented at Princeton University in 2002, it has since been presented as part of a number of exhibitions including the 2nd International Architecture Biennale in Rotterdam in 2005. The project proposes a 195-hectare landscape intended to float just beneath the ocean's surface. Designed as a replacement for the Diablo Canyon nuclear plant when its 40-year license expires in 2026, the project suggests wave power as an alternative to traditional energy sources. The project was inspired by the energy crisis in California as evidenced by the rolling black-outs that affected millions of people across the state in 2000 and 2001.

Working with scientists at Princeton University, Obuchi was able to experiment with ceramic crystals, a hard but flexible material that deforms when an electric current passes through it. The mechanical stress on the material produces an electric charge known as piezo-electricity that was discovered by Pierre and Jacques Curie in the 1880s and is similar in principle to the spark generated by the gas lighter on a stove.

The Wave Garden consists of 1,734 ceramic tiles that are each 7.6 centimetres thick, linked together and supported on the water's surface by tubular buoys. During the week, the motion of the ocean's waves causes the flexible tiles to bend and generate energy through piezoelectricity. Usage of the power the Wave Garden supplies during the week determines its shape on the weekend, when energy consumption decreases. "I was interested in finding a way to investigate new relationships between architecture and society that go beyond the urban scale of a project but tap into our cultural life", says Obuchi of his innovative concept. If Californians consume less energy during the week, they are rewarded on the weekends. The tiles rise to the surface to create a parkscape with swimming pools. However, if they consume large amounts of energy during the week, the Wave Garden stays submerged during the weekend while it works to recoup energy. Obuche notes that his interest lay in discovering "potential patterns of water and cultural movement generated by energy consumption as a new way of thinking about the environment."

His proposal is a response to the potential surplus power generated by power plants. "Power plants never shut down so the energy they produce is always constant whatever the demand", he notes, referring to the reduced amount of energy required at night or on weekends. "This urban scale device transforms the surplus energy for use for cultural or leisure activities." Prompting us to take note of our energy consumption, Obuche's project also points to the possibilities inherent in dynamic rather than static interaction.

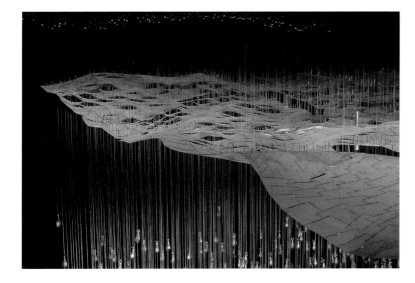

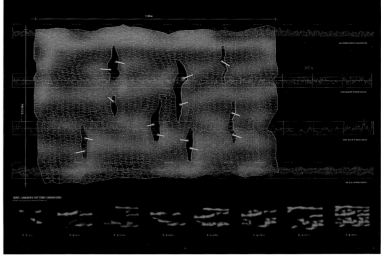

The grid of floating membranes while being charged with power create a series of undulating islands for recreational use.

The model shows the surface consisting of 1,734 ceramic-tiled membranes, powered by a computational interactive system.

Plan view of one of the floating membranes measuring 1.2 x 1.6 kilometre. The diagram indicates the possible configuration of the occupiable surface as a marine park.

left: Site plan of proposed "Wave Garden" located adjacent to Diablo Canyon nuclear power plant in California.

The islands as they would be seen by visitors during the weekend when the "Wave Garden" transforms into a marine park.

Ex Arsenale Conference Centre | Stefano Boeri Architetti

COMPLETION
2009

LOCATION
La Maddalena, Italy

DESIGN TEAM
Stefano Boeri with Michele Brunello, Davor Popovic, Barbara Cadeddu,
2+1 Officina Architettura, Vincenzo Vella, Liverani/Molteni Architetti,
Marco Brega (design)
Javier Deferrari, Andrea Grippo, Eugenio Feresin, Marco Tradori,
Costantina Verzì, Marco Dessì, Marco Giorgio, Daniele Barillari,
Mario Bastianelli, Maurizio Burragato, Andrea Barbierato (project team)

STRUCTURAL ENGINEERING
Italingegneria; Enetec

CLIENT
Department for Civil Protection and Region of Sardinia

Originally commissioned to host the 2009 G8 Summit, which was re-located to L'Aquila in central Italy following the Abruzzo earthquake in April 2009, the complex of buildings on a former military arsenal on the island of Sardinia is now home to a new complex of buildings and a marina. Designed by Milan-based Stefano Boeri Architetti, the project's underlying aim was to reinvigorate this abandoned site, which enjoys a privileged location on the Mediterranean Sea and yet was blighted by a 100-year-old history of heavy use by the military. "The recovery of an area, a site of large symbolic value to the local inhabitants and equally marked by its military stigma, presented enormous and multi-faceted challenges", explains Boeri. However, "The opportunity to intervene in a location of exceptional natural beauty offered enormous possibilities. Our goal was to minimize the effects of new construction in respect of the natural landscape."

The project posed manifold concerns, not least of all the clean-up of the site, which required two ships removing earth contaminated by oil and paraffin from the site daily over a period of two months. The site also warranted the removal and treatment of 70,000 tonnes of polluted land that contained residues of iron, carbon and exhausted oils, and 380 tonnes of asbestos.

Once completed, the master plan for the 155,000-square-metre site, will make every effort to orient new buildings, intercepted by historical buildings that have been renovated, around a series of interconnected public spaces that line the harbour front. In an effort to transform the area into a site of commercial and consumer interests, as well as to instigate activities for tourists and the local community, a series of buildings for multiple functions of all scales were determined. These included an exhibition venue, a hotel, a sailing school, a sports and wellness centre, office spaces, cafés and restaurants, as well as a harbour which can comfortably accommodate 700 boats. The hope is that the mix of spaces will attract people to this waterfront location throughout the day and into the evening, ensuring it becomes an active extension of La Maddalena, a town on an island of the same name at the northern end of Sardinia.

This careful arrangement is anchored by the most visually compelling of the projects, the conference centre, whose perforated façade cantilevers over the site like a giant fishing cage thrown out from a trawler. The linear lower level is a monolith made from basalt stone,

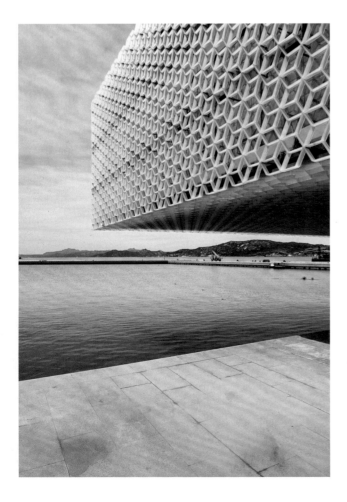

Detail view of the Ex Arsenale Conference Centre and its direct relationship to the Mediterranean Sea.

top right: Exterior view of the Ex Arsenale Conference Centre, which cantilevers over the water.

bottom right: Detail view of the steel latticework that covers the upper floor, affixed to the building with cable trusses. The latticework is both a decorative feature as well as functional, providing sunshade to the exposed façade of the building.

acting as a structural support to the upper level, which is more than double the space of the lower floor, at 420 square metres, and is flanked by a steel lattice-work structure affixed to the building with cable trusses. This architectural detail on the one hand provides a decorative element to the otherwise straightforward construction, and on the other functions as a sunshade for this exposed façade. Inside, the open-plan space has been divided into rooms for smaller and larger gatherings, each of which has views through to the water. As Boeri notes, the building's distinctive design "reacts with the sun and different light conditions so that its character is constantly changing. At night, the light irradiates from the interior, converting the building into a lantern suspended between land and sea."

In addition to using seawater in the service of the heating and cooling systems of the building, renewable energy is provided by solar panels and photovoltaic surfaces on the roofs of buildings. Green roofs on some of the buildings also help to control heat levels, and rainwater is collected and filtered for use in water reserves and in the hotel bathrooms, for example. Keen to apply as many green elements as possible, these interventions help realize a sustainable design that is in tune with the project's overall aim to preserve the natural biodiversity of the site. As Boeri states, although the plan was envisioned for the G8 summit, the "Underlying idea was always wider in scope." Providing both opportunities for tourism and economic expansion, the project aims to take its place among other key reference points of new development along the Mediterranean coast that are transforming these centuries-old sites of civilization with new uses and social landscapes.

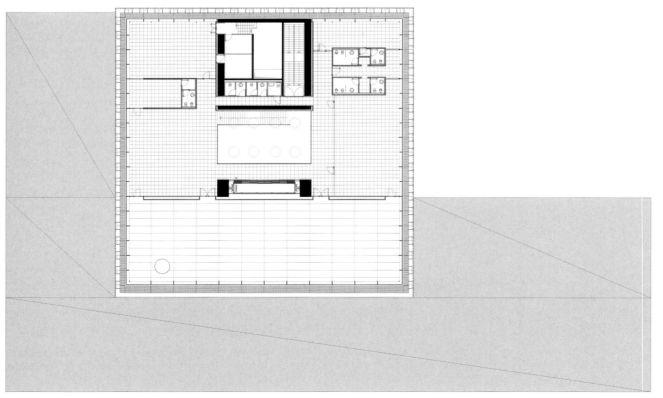

First floor plan

WISA Wooden Design Hotel | Pieta-Linda Auttila

COMPLETION
2009

LOCATION
Helsinki, Finland

DESIGN TEAM
Pieta-Linda Auttila (design)

STRUCTURAL ENGINEERING
Tero Sundberg; Hannu Hirsi

CLIENT
UMP-Kymmene Timber

Designing a building in 24 hours, complete with construction documents, might seem challenging enough, but the project to conceive a new hotel for Helsinki's South Harbour came complete with additional difficulties. These included the lack of access by road so that all the construction materials had to be brought to the site via boat, in addition to the location of the project on a rocky islet at the mercy of unpredictable weather. And yet, these drawbacks did not stop 100 architects entering the WISA 24h Wooden Design Workshop, a competition that sought inventive designs for an approximately 30–40-square-metre wooden building. Organized by sustainable forestry company UPM to exploit the potential of recyclable Finnish woods, the winning design by Pieta-Linda Auttila, an interior architect who graduated from the University of Art and Design Helsinki in 2009, responds to the natural setting with a sculptural form that draws inspiration from drift wood found washed up on the beach. "I loved the very open and conceptual topic of the project", says Auttila while she admits that "the logistics were demanding." Built in three sections, the hotel incorporates two guest rooms separated by a central atrium that is open to the elements.

In contrast to the angular forms of the pine guest rooms that sit at opposite edges of the site, the billowing lengths of slatted birch plywood that provide a canopy over a central communal space are reminiscent of a boat's sail fluttering in the wind. Auttila was able to construct the design with the help of five professional carpenters who used 8-millimetre-thick planks of birch, which they submerged in water until saturated, then molded into the desired shapes and eventually joined to the structural planes of the guesthouses with additional layers of plywood for support. "I was interested in using techniques drawn from the boat-building industry", notes Auttila, "as a way to connect to the conceptual theme of the competition and as a response to the waterfront setting." Although expertly constructed, Auttila acknowledges that compromises were needed to realize the complex design. These included the use of vertical ceiling supports for the central canopy. "It was impossible to build scaffolding that was high enough on the rocks, and with the strong wind, to make the supports less visible", she explains. However, given the challenges to the design, the high level of craftsmanship is evident in the resultant vocabulary of forms that characterize this isolated retreat. The open form of the central atrium is in contrast to the closed boxes of the guest houses, and yet these are both oriented towards the water and framed on two sides by floor-to-ceiling glass panel, providing views across the water to the city of Helsinki.

In a country where three-quarters of the land area is covered by forest, experimental projects such as the WISA workshop help determine innovative concepts that foster progressive thinking and fresh responses to building with this traditional material. Taking up the challenge, Auttila asserts, "I have always been interested in finding new ways to use familiar materials."

Rear view of the WISA Wooden Design Hotel in Helsinki's South Harbour.

The discrete side entrance to the hotel, made from a wood plank construction, is located on the water's edge.

The floor-to-ceiling glazed front façade of the WISA Design Hotel provides a porthole-like window onto the water.

top right: The curvilinear slatted wood canopies that frame the open-air terraces are in contrast to the rectilinear form of the main living spaces, giving the impression of waves crashing against the building, inspired by the coastal setting.

bottom right: Interior view of the WISA Design Hotel. A glass partition ensures that the interior and exterior living spaces of the hotel are physically and visually integrated and that views to the water are maintained throughout the living spaces, emphasizing the distinctive location of the hotel.

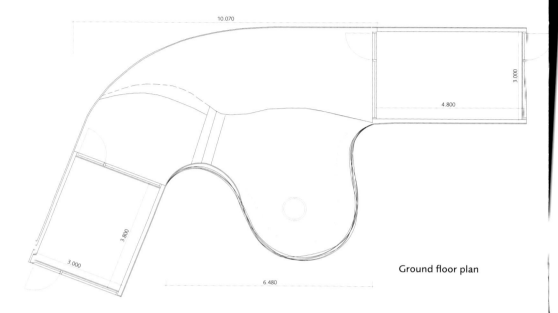

Ground floor plan

Index

Illustration Credits

Cover photograph:
Gustavo Frittegotto

8 ©iStockphoto.com/Mark Burrows
9T ©Olafur Eliasson, 2008, courtesy of
the artist and Public Art Fund
9C Oliver Kleinschmidt
9B Zoë Ryan
10L The Art Institute of Chicago
10R ©iStockphoto.com/Nickos
11L ©iStockphoto.com/S. Greg Panosian
11R ©iStockphoto.com/godrick
11C ©iStockphoto.com/
Andrew Kazmierski
11B The Estate of Gordon Matta-Clark
and David Zwirner, New York
13L Real Estate Webmasters
13TR Brynjar Gunnarsson
13BL ©iStockphoto.com/jhgrigg
14T Architecture Research Office
14C, 14B UrbanLab
15 Balmori Associates
16 Architecture Research Office
17 Stan Allen Architect
19 Arup
23, 26-27 Dieter Grau
24, 37 Atelier Dreiseitl
28 WSDOT
29L ELBE&FLUT
HafenCity Hamburg GmbH
29R Jeff Boggess
30 Fotofrizz, HafenCity Hamburg GmbH
31 Oliver Kleinschmidt
34-35 Foster + Partners, Atelier Dreiseitl
36 A Dawn Journal
41 ©iStockphoto.com/
Hanoded Photography/
42R ©iStockphoto.com
Marc Slingerland
42L Rob Lengkeek
43 DuraVermeer
44 Dutch Ministry of Infrastructure
and Water Management
45 DuraVermeer
47 William Veerbeek
48 Baca Architects
51L ©iStockphoto.com/rusm
51R David M. Heald
52L Tadao Ando
52R Chichu Art Museum/
Mitsumasa Fujitsuka
53L Groninger Museum/
Marten de Leeuw
53R Michel Denancé
54T Beat Widmer, courtesy of
Diller Scofidio+Renfro
54B Courtesy of Diller Scofidio+Renfro
55L Christian Richters
55R Jo Reid and John Peck
56L Christian Richters
56C Program Collective/Olga Subirós
56R Program Collective
57T arena Berlin
57BL ©iStockphoto.com/rusm
57BR ©iStockphoto.com
58L Jonathan Kirschenfeld Associates
58R Javier González-Campaña
59L SHoP Architects

59R courtesy of Kiriaty Architects
and Aqua Creation
60T Margherita Spiluttini
60B Edmund Sumner
61 Klaus-Peter Gast
62TL ©iStockphoto.com/Seastones
Photography
62TR ©iStockphoto.com/GTMedia
Services
62CL ©iStockphoto.comAlbert Speelman
62 C ©iStockphoto.com/Uschools
University Images (Imperial Palace)
62CR ©iStockphoto.com/aschlabach
62B ©iStockphoto.com/ileximage
64 Julius Shulman
65 courtesy of the
Western Pennsylvania Conservancy
66TLR, 66C RO-VORM, Amsterdam
66B Christian Richters
67L Greg Lynn FORM
67R Edmund Carter, Nikita Shah,
Ashvin Bhargava
68L Stacey Thomas, Tina Jelenc, Chintan
Raveshia, Florian Heinzelmann
68R Satoru Mishima
69L Kawatetsu
69R Roderick Coyne/Alsop and Partners
70L Paul Warchol
70R Waterstudio.nl
73-75 MOS Architects
77 Steve Turner
78 Steven Holl Architects
79, 80T, 81 Paul Warchol
80B Michael Van Valkenburg
83-87 Willem Franken
89 Bart van Damme
91T Guido Merkelbach
91L Bart van Damme
91R Fernando Herrera
93-95 Paul Tahon and Ronan
and Erwan Bouroullec
97-99 Stijn Brakkee and Daria Scagliola
100 Harry Schiffer
101T Elvira Klamminger
101B Simone Jeska
103 Herzog & de Meuron
104T Alexandra Gärtner
104B Gertrud Kanu
105 Herzog & de Meuron
106-107 OMA
(Office for Metropolitan Architecture)
108-109 UN Studio
111-113 BIG and JDS Architects
114-117 Åke Eison Lindman
118-119 Andy Stagg
121 Zaha Hadid Architects
123 Nic LeHoux
124, 125T Diller Scofidio+Renfro
125B Nic LeHoux
126 Nic LeHoux
127 Iwan Baan
128-132 Statsbygg
133 Oliver Kleinschmidt
135-139 Adam Mørk
© Henning Larsen Architects
141-143 MASS Studies
145-147 IwamotoScott Architecture
148-149 Yusuke Obuchi

150-153 Paolo Rosselli
155-157 Arno de la Chapelle, UPM

The Authors

Zoë Ryan studied art history at the University of Sussex, the University of Amsterdam and Hunter College, City University of New York where she received her master's degree. She is the Neville Bryan Curator of Design at The Art Institute of Chicago where she is responsible for organizing exhibitions and building the museum's first collection of contemporary design. Ryan was a curatorial assistant at the Museum of Modern Art, New York and at The Victoria & Albert Museum, London, and subsequently became Senior Curator at the Van Alen Institute (VAI) in New York, a non-profit public art and architecture organization where she organized the exhibition "The Good Life: New Public Spaces of Recreation", installed on Pier 40 in New York City. Her writing on art and design has been published internationally. She is currently an Adjunct Assistant Professor at the School of Art and Design at the University of Illinois at Chicago.

Chris Zevenbergen studied ecology at the Agricultural University Wageningen and received his doctorate in environmental engineering from the University Utrecht. He is a professor at the Water Engineering Department of UNESCO-IHE (Institute for Water Education) in Delft. He is also director of the Business Development Department of DuraVermeer Group NV, a real estate developer. He is co-founder and chairman of the European Network COST C22 on urban flood management and the Flood Resilience Group (FRG). His research area is environmental engineering and water management, with a particular focus on integrated approaches to manage floods in urban environments.

Dieter Grau is a gardener and accredited landscape architect. Since 1994, he has been working for Atelier Dreiseitl, Überlingen, Germany. Atelier Dreiseitl specializes in river restoration projects, water features, large-scale water management schemes and the integration of watercycles in buildings or urban quarters. In 1996 he became head of the Landscape Architecture Department there. He is now a partner in the office and is involved in projects around the world. He lectures frequently worldwide.

Zeljka Carol Kekez holds a master's degree in business administration and a graduate certificate in urban design. Pursuing a doctoral programme in urban studies and planning, her area of interest is urban identity and place making with a focus on waterfront environments. She worked for the landscape architecture office Walker Macy, Portland, Oregon and various other design firms, directing business development with clients worldwide. Zeljka Carol Kekez is a principal at Atelier Dreiseitl responsible for strategic planning and global business operations.

Acknowledgements

For helping me in the making of this publication, I would like to thank the designers, architects, landscape architects, artists, their inspired clients and the photographers featured in this publication for their innovative work, cooperation and generosity. All quotes unless otherwise indicated were obtained through interviews that I conducted between 2007 and 2010 with many practitioners and experts who graciously gave their time, insights and knowledge to this project, enriching its content far beyond what I could have achieved alone. Many thanks to Oliver Kleinschmidt for his commitment to this project, which resulted in the elegant graphic design. Special thanks also to Dieter Grau, Zeljka Carol Kekez and Chris Zevenbergen for their perceptive essays on the potential and challenges of building on, by and with water. I am indebted to Raymond W. Gastil, formerly director of the Van Alen Institute in New York and director of city planning for Manhattan and Seattle for encouraging my interest in the intersection between architecture and water. I would also like to acknowledge Paul Lewis, Marc Tsurumaki and David J. Lewis of New York-based architecture studio Lewis.Tsurumaki.Lewis's exhibition "Architecture + Water" held at the Van Alen Institute in 2001 prompted my initial explorations, which eventually led to this volume. Finally, heartfelt thanks to editor Ria Stein for her passionate support of this project and her astute editing and expert guidance.